Table of Contents

Introduction - *How to use this book*

The purpose of *The Basics of Golf Clubmaking* is to acquaint golfers the world over with another enjoyable and profitable aspect of this great game of golf. For the golfer who is naturally inquisitive, who enjoys tinkering, or who just wants to embark on something fun and different, Golfsmith has opened the door with *The Basics of Golf Clubmaking*.

If you want to start a craft where you can assemble your own custom set of golf clubs; where you can experiment inexpensively with different grips, shafts or clubheads; and where your clubmaking skills can actually improve your golf game, then *The Basics of Golf Clubmaking* was written for you.

At the same time, golf clubmaking can help you earn extra money – by assembling and repairing clubs for others. Many of the smallest and largest golf club repair shops in the United States and several of the so-called major golf clubmaking companies got their start with Golfsmith in just this fashion.

Today's crowded golf courses are evidence of golf's growing popularity and a corresponding open market for products and services. It is estimated that there are as many as 30 million golfers in the United States today, with the number expected to continue to grow.

Can you imagine operating a business that brings you in contact with golfers of every skill level? Better still, can you imagine operating a business where your customers are "nuts" – golf nuts, that is? Can you imagine operating a business where your customers love each and every new product and truly appreciate everything you can do for them? Golf clubmaking is just such a business, and for many it has grown into a full-time profession that allows its proprietors to work in a field they truly love – GOLF.

Whether you are starting out in the bedroom of your apartment, your basement or your garage, *The Basics of Golf Clubmaking* is designed to start you on the road toward a better golf game, an enjoyable and rewarding craft, and if you choose, a profitable business. It is a presentation of the basics involved in assembling golf clubs, written for golfer 's of all skill levels, from weekend duffer to pro. It contains step-by-step instructions for regripping golf clubs, and assembling putters, irons, wedges, metal woods. If you can safely use the most common tools and follow the procedures shown in each chapter, *The Basics of Golf Clubmaking* will enable you to assemble top-quality golf clubs that can improve your game and increase your enjoyment of golf.

At some point you may be ready to expand your horizons, by including custom clubfitting as a service in your golf clubmaking and club repair business. *Golfsmith's Practical Clubfitting Program* by Tom Wishon, our chief technical officer, is the golf industry's definitive guide to finding the optimum set of clubs for any golfer. It is the most comprehensive book of its kind, with over 440 pages and literally hundreds of graphs, charts, photos and illustrations.

The Basics of Golf Clubmaking

Copyright © 1989 by Golfsmith International, Inc.
Revised © 1999 by Golfsmith International, Inc.
2nd Reprint © 1999

3rd Reprint © 2002

ISBN 0-913563-04-8

This book was designed and produced by Golfsmith International, Inc.

Published in the United States of America
by Golfsmith International, Inc.
11000 North IH-35
Austin, TX 78753
1-800-456-3344 • (512) 837-4810

Edited by

Russell Caver

John Hunt

Photography by

David Stockwell

Design & Illustration by

Donny Ray

Printed in the United States of America

Golfsmith International started in 1967 in the bedroom of an apartment and later moved up to the "big time" when the company relocated to the basement of a house. Golfsmith was the first company to recognize that golf club assembly is a craft that is accessible by people from all walks of life.

Since its founding, Golfsmith has been the leader in the components supply segment of the golf industry, growing to more than 1,000 employees. The company each day ships up to 10,000 packages containing items including grips, shafts, clubheads, golf bags, golf shoes, golf apparel and complete clubs from its location in Austin, Texas. It occupies a 41-acre campus with more than 300,000 square feet under roof, and also operates a growing national network of golf superstores, all of which carry an extensive line of clubmaking components. The company also operates a golf clubmaking factory, a full-range golf club repair facility, and a golf club repair training program. Golfsmith's headquarters site includes a fully-equipped Learning and Club Testing Facility, with an 80-station practice range and a staff of more than 20 golf professionals.

The company attributes its successful growth to its employees. By hiring people who have a special enthusiasm for golf, Golfsmith has built an international reputation for outstanding services and superior products that are helping golfers of all skill levels to improve their golf games.

Golfsmith takes pride in knowing that it has helped hundreds of businesses get started and that literally tens of thousands of golf enthusiasts derive their source of enjoyment from golf clubmaking. The company has grown and been successful because its customers have also been successful in their own clubmaking pursuits.

In addition to its nationwide toll-free telephone order line (1-800-456-3344), Golfsmith maintains a customer service number (1-800-925-7709), which is staffed by experienced employees who can answer questions about the procedures in this book. The customer service line should also be used for questions about Golfsmith services and products including special clubmaking supplies, parts, or tools, and any clubmaking or clubfitting procedures requiring technical assistance or expertise. Golfsmith's goal is to help you succeed, and we work hard to give you the best service and best assistance in the golf industry.

To paraphrase the late Ben Hogan, those of us at Golfsmith cannot wait for the next day to get here so we can get started working in golf again! It is our goal to help you to feel this same enthusiasm for golf.

Chapter 1
Fundamentals

Welcome to the world of golf club assembly. You are about to embark on a very enjoyable and rewarding activity. In fact, most people who participate in club building will tell you they enjoy this aspect of the game almost as much, and in some cases, more than playing.

The one thing you will find in the pages that follow is how simple the task of assembling a golf club can be. It does not require a significant investment in tools and supplies, nor does it require a lot of space. Many of the tools needed are those you probably already have around the house, such as a hacksaw, a heavy duty knife, a hammer, a file or sand paper, a tape measure of some kind and, if you have a work bench, a standard bench vise. While there are some specialty tools that can simplify certain tasks, the basic tools will put you well on your way.

The Basics of Golf Clubmaking shows you not only the procedures for assembling golf clubs, but also the use of the tools needed to make the job easier. Each section lists the tools and supplies required to complete a specific task, along with options that you may find helpful. Stock numbers are listed for all of the tools and supplies featured in this book and each is available in the annual Golfsmith Clubmaking Catalog. Of course, the more tools you want, the more money it will cost. We recommend that you start slowly with the basics and at your own pace. You can get an incredible amount of enjoyment and satisfaction out of the basic assembly shown in this book. And, when your friends see how well the clubs YOU built play, they will want you to assemble THEIR next set of clubs.

One of the biggest advantages of building new golf clubs from components is the overall cost savings. Year after year it seems that prices for fully assembled golf clubs get higher and higher with the cost of some of the "latest and greatest" clubs reaching as much as $500 for a single driver and several thousand dollars for a set of irons. Putters and wedges are not immune from these inflated prices either, with the hottest models costing more than $100 and as much as $200 At these prices, the question the consumer must ask is, "am I getting a better game?" While the answer may be yes, you need to determine if the benefits justify the costs.

By comparison, you can build yourself a high-quality, stainless steel iron with a premium steel shaft and rubber composition grip for around $20. Even with a high-quality graphite shaft, the cost of an iron can be less than $50. A titanium driver constructed with one of the most popular premium graphite shafts on the market will cost only around $150. Built correctly, following the procedures outlined in this book, these clubs will perform as well, and many times better, than the expensive "name brand" clubs currently on the market.

The cost savings and the results themselves make this a very rewarding and enjoyable hobby. You may find that you can even make a little money and provide your friends with high-quality equipment that will cost them substantially less than they imagined.

GOLF CLUB ASSEMBLY 101

This book illustrates the mechanical steps you need to follow when assembling a golf club. However, before you begin cutting, epoxying and gripping, there are few things you need to know about making the club fit. All clubs are not the same, nor are the players that use them. It is a constant sense of amazement to see people of all shapes and sizes trying to use the same kind of equipment. We do not all wear the same pant size, shirt size or hat size, so why should we play the same club size? Maybe that is a bad analogy. This is golf, not clothing. After all, Tiger Woods probably plays off-the-rack clubs, just as Mark McGuire uses a bat from his local sporting goods store, and Pete Sampras uses a racket he got off-the-rack at his local tennis pro shop. Right? WRONG. These professional athletes all have their tools-of-the-trade custom fit for their specific needs. But, just because you are not a professional does not mean you won't benefit from custom-fit clubs. As a matter of fact, the average golfer often benefits more from custom-fit clubs than does a professional.

Fitting Fundamentals

Several decisions must be made before the assembly begins. First, determine what the player is trying to accomplish. What are their goals? What do they want out of their new club or clubs? Of course, if you are building the club for yourself, you must ask yourself these questions. By following the series of steps outlined below, you will find that the process is not too complicated.

Step 1: Determining the golfers goals, wants and needs.

The first task is to assess what you or the player you are building the club for wants to accomplish with the new club or clubs. Maybe the desire is to hit the ball farther (who doesn't) or straighter. Maybe it is just a matter of wanting to use the latest technology in golf clubs, hoping something about it will improve your game. Whatever the reason, decide what your goals are before moving on.

Step 2: Evaluating current golf clubs.

It is very important to evaluate the current clubs being used and the kinds of shots they produce. Note the specifications that you like and want to duplicate in the new club or clubs. Club evaluation forms, available in the Golfsmith Clubmaking Catalog (Stock #8844), help guide you on the specifications to check. An example of these forms is listed in the Appendix. The main things for which to look: the materials of the club or clubs, the length, the loft and lie angle of the club, the shaft flex, the weight and swingweight of the clubs, and the grip style and size. Once these specifications are determined, you can better see where changes may need to be made.

Step 3: Measurements

Measuring yourself for a golf club is a lot easier than measuring yourself for a new suit of clothes. Measuring for club length is usually a good place to start. Golfsmith recommends measuring the wrist-to-floor length, using a 48-inch Club Rule (Stock #8460). Simply stand straight, with arms and hands hanging down to the side, and place the ruler alongside. Note the distance from the wrist to the floor (see photo 1-1). Use the natural crease at the base of the hand as the point of reference for the wrist. Measure both right- and left-hand sides and if the measurements are slightly different, simply use the average of the two. The charts on 109 show the recommended finished club lengths based on wrist-to-floor measurements. This should be used as a guide only. Note that these recommended lengths are in ranges and not specific length recommendations. This is because other factors must be considered. The player's physical ability and strength, along with their golfing ability, should be factored into the length decision. Longer clubs are harder to hit than shorter clubs for most people, so the ability of the player to hit longer clubs must be considered. Finally, and most importantly, is the comfort of the player. The player should be comfortable with the length of the clubs they are playing.

Golfsmith recommends players play the longest club they can control. Control is the key word here. Control, in this sense, is defined as the longest club a player can hit in the center of the face a high percentage of the time for their ability. The reason for longer clubs is simple: longer clubs enhance the potential for a slight increase in clubhead speed, which can result in increased distance. Understand that a longer club does not automatically mean longer shots, but the potential is there if the ball is struck in the center of the clubface.

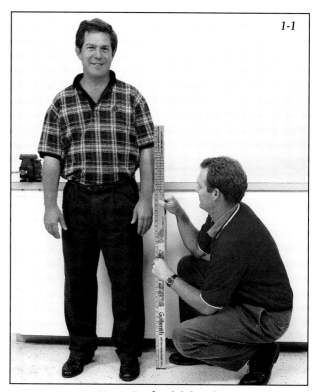

1-1

Measuring for club length

The player's physical ability and strength, along with their golfing ability, should be factored into the length decision.

Effects of Incorrect Lie Angle

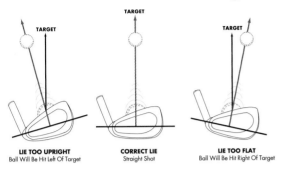

Diagram 1-1

The lie of the club, or the way the sole of the club contacts the ground during the swing, is another important factor, especially for irons. This lie angle of a club can influence the accuracy of shots, especially in the shorter irons. (see Diagram 1-1) Experienced clubfitters use the term "Dynamic Lie Fitting" when referring to the proper way to determine the correct lie of a club for a player. The "Dynamic" part of this term means that the club must be swung by the player, preferably striking a ball, from a surface that will leave a mark on the sole of the club. Golfsmith's Lie Test Board (Stock #4990), shown in photo 1-2, leaves a removable mark on the sole of a club, indicating where the sole contacted the ground during a swing. The Dynamic Lie Angle Test Platform is a heavy-duty, adjustable lie-testing device that is used by many professional clubfitters to fit the dynamic lie (see photo 1-2a). To determine the proper lie on irons, simply have a player hit a shot off the lie board or some similar surface that will leave a mark on the sole of the club. Golfsmith recommends taping the sole of the club with masking tape as shown in photo 1-3. As seen in this photo, contacting the lie boards will make a distinctive mark or tear in the tape on the sole. The black mark in the photo indicates the center of the sole and is used as the point of reference. For every ¼ inch off the centerline the sole mark is, a one-degree lie adjustment is needed. Reference the center mark of the sole. If the mark is towards the toe of the club, the lie angle is too flat for the player. If the mark is towards the heel of the club, the lie angle is too upright for the player. Incorrect lie angles can have a major effect on accuracy in the short irons, with the effect diminishing as the loft decreases and length of the club increases. After performing a dynamic lie test on just one club, usually a 5-iron or a 7-iron, you can progress the lie angle one degree through the set, moving from, for example, 56 degrees in a 1-iron to 65 degrees in a sand wedge. See the specification chart in the Appendix on page 110 for standard lie specifications.

The loft angle of a golf club is the specification that has the most influence on the trajectory of the ball. In most cases, especially with irons, loft adjustments are not usually necessary unless the player has a very clear cut need to either increase or decrease the trajectory of their shots. Irons will have a progression of lofts throughout the set, which dictate, along with the length of the club, the length and trajectory of the shot. With woods, especially drivers, there are a wide variety of lofts available to meet just about any trajectory need. However, metal wood lofts cannot be adjusted, so choose carefully. The loft of a wood is the main factor in determining the trajectory the ball will travel. It is important to note, however, that the lower the loft on a wood, the more difficult it is to hit the ball straight. If you have a lower swing speed, more loft is usually beneficial. The higher the swing speed, the lower the loft a player can usually use and still achieve the desired trajectory. See charts on page 110 for a list of the average loft specifications for irons, woods and putters.

With club shafts, it is easier to make the selection if you know the swing speed of the player. There are several devices on the market that measure swing speed. However, these are not absolutely necessary. There are charts that estimate a player's swing speed based on the shot-carry distance of specific clubs. See the shaft selection segment of this chapter on page 11 for a look at the distance carry/swing speed chart.

1-3

Incorrect lie angles can have a major effect on accuracy in the short irons, with the effect diminishing as the loft decreases and length of the club increases.

1-4

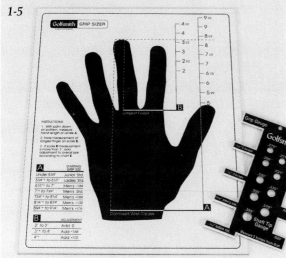

1-5

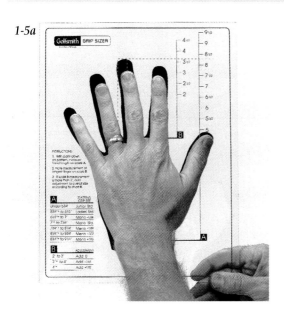

1-5a

One other basic element of clubfitting is grip size. The grip is where the player connects with the club and how that connection is made can have an impact on the performance and feel of the club. One method of determining the appropriate grip size is the fingertip-to-palm method. Photo 1-4 shows how, if fit properly, the fingers of the left hand (for a right-handed player) barely touch the palm portion of the hand. Another method is to use a grip sizer like the one shown in photo 1-5 (Stock #937). To use, simply place the player's hand on the sizer as shown in photo 1-5a and reference the chart on the sizer. The chart will indicate the correct grip size. If oversized grips are indicated, refer to page 112 in the Appendix of this book for taping instructions.

There are other aspects of clubfitting to be considered. Here, we have tried to touch on the basics to help you build a better-fitted club. For a more in-depth look at clubfitting, we recommend reading *The Golfsmith Practical Clubfitting Program* book (Stock #8500). This program concentrates on the specifications of a club that, if changed, have a direct and immediate effect on the feel of the club and the ball flight a club produces.

Step 4: Swing Analysis

It is not critical for you to have a full knowledge of the golf swing, but it is important to understand your own swing, and if fitting others, be able to recognize a few basic things about the swing. Usually, the better the player the better their basic knowledge of the golf swing. If you do not have a good, basic knowledge of the golf swing, you will need to develop one. There are numerous resources at your disposal to help you increase your understanding of the golf swing, including: your golf pro, your own practice and play, books and articles about the golf swing, and the PGA or LPGA Tour pros on television. Study the commentators' analysis on PGA players on tournament telecasts. Read the instruction articles in golf magazines. The important thing to understand is that if the ball slices or hooks or goes straight, the vast majority of the time it is due to something the player does, not the club itself.

Step 5: Fitting Decisions

After you have gone through the basic fitting steps outlined here look over the charts and fitting forms in the Appendix. Now you're almost ready. The next step: selecting the golf club components.

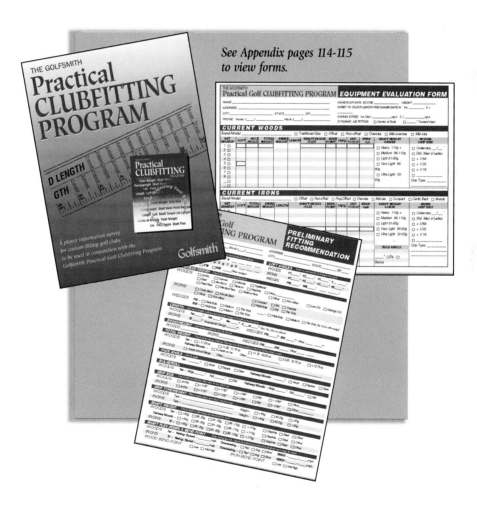

WHERE TO START - SIFTING THROUGH THE OPTIONS

Making a purchasing decision on golf clubs can be a daunting task. There are literally hundreds of brands

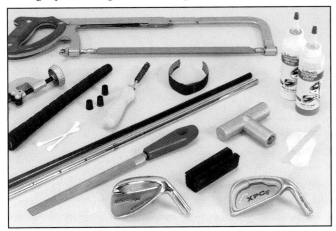

and styles, all claiming to dramatically improve your game. The truth is, there are certain specifications in a golf club that impact the way a ball will fly and the way a club feels. Matching the right specifications to the individual is the key ingredient to ensuring that the clubs chosen will produce the best ball flight and the best feel possible. So, how do you decide? Let's take a look at each of the components in a club and the key factors to consider.

Supplies for Iron and Wedge Heads

CLUBHEADS

In the Golfsmith Clubmaking Catalog, there are multiple iron and metal wood head options. There are also many wedge and putter head options. All of the clubheads have different features designed to provide specific benefits to specific players. Finding the features each player prefers, matching the specifications through custom fitting and, last but not least, finding the cosmetics the player likes best are the key elements to selecting the right clubhead. See page 111 in the Appendix outlining common clubhead design features and terminology.

Iron Heads - Selection

The features of iron heads today seem to be much more complex and diverse than they used to be. In the past, most iron heads looked pretty much the same. Today, there are many different types of blade designs, cavity-back designs, multi-metal designs and so on. Keep in mind that more flash does not necessarily mean more benefit and that the benefits of any particular design feature are pretty basic. Today's "game improvement" features are designed for the majority of golfers who hope to get some help from their equipment when their swing fails them. Iron heads with this type of design are usually larger than traditional-sized irons, feature a cavity back with added weighting in the heel and toe, and incorporate added weighting in the sole. While commonly referred to as "game improvement" features, all types of players play them — from touring pros to beginners. The majority of these clubheads are manufactured by a process called investment casting. This means the material from which the clubheads are made is invested or poured into a mold, and when cooled produces a solid part. Many investment cast clubheads are made from 431 stainless steel, 15-5 stainless steel or 17-4 stainless steel. These materials are selected for their durability, price and ability to have specifications altered for custom-fitting purposes.

New technology and materials have come to the forefront in recent years that allow designers to use space-aged material, such as titanium, to produce new single-, bi- and even tri-material clubheads. These new material combinations enable golf club designers to expand the parameters of the design process to help improve the performance and playability of each clubhead. For instance, designers can enhance perimeter weighting, a game improvement feature, by combining lighter materials with heavier materials. Some of the new perimeter-weighting options available to the modern club designer include: stainless steel heads with titanium inserts, stainless steel heads with beryllium-copper inserts, titanium heads with brass inserts, and aluminum heads with tungsten and stainless inserts. While there are no definitive studies to demonstrate that these new designs offer superior playability, the greater flexibility in weight distribution is viewed by some as a real advancement in game-improvement technology. The decision that ultimately must be made is whether these high-tech materials and their benefits are worth the higher prices.

Other processes and materials, such as forged-carbon-steel iron clubheads, are still available and preferred by some lower handicappers and golf traditionalists. Previously, most forged-carbon-steel clubheads were "muscle-back" designs. More recently, cavity-back designs have emerged in forged-carbon-steel clubheads. These carbon-steel clubheads are generally softer than most of the stainless-steel clubheads used in investment-cast clubheads. To some players, this softer material gives the club a softer feel. However, the forging process is more labor-intensive and thus, produces a more expensive clubhead than most pure stainless steel clubheads. The forged process involves heating the carbon steel and hammering — or "forging" — it into the shape of the iron clubhead. Placing the two halves of the mold (upper and lower) into a special forging press, the steel is hammered into the shape of the head. Finally, forged carbon-steel clubheads are readily adaptable for custom-fitting purposes because the carbon steel is easier to bend and manipulate than most stainless steel clubheads.

Once the clubhead design and material is selected and the loft, lie and weight specifications fall within the standard range, the decision becomes largely cosmetic. Pick a clubhead that appeals to you, regardless of the rationale. Believe it or not, your comfort with the look of the club can have an impact on club performance.

Wood Head Materials - Selection

Wood clubheads, more specifically metal wood clubheads, have changed dramatically over the years. While some die-hard golfers still prefer "wood" clubheads, the overwhelming majority of today's golfers play with some sort of metal wood head. Stainless steel has been the predominant material used to manufacturer metal wood heads since they burst onto the modern market approximately 25 years ago.

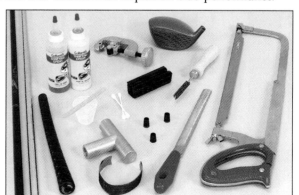

Supplies for Wood Heads

Since then, numerous materials, most notably titanium, have been used to produce clubheads with features that could not be incorporated into clubs with stainless steel or wood. The most evident difference you see in a titanium head is its size. Because titanium is lighter than stainless, the head can be made larger, but not heavier. These new materials have introduced a multitude of bi–, tri- and quad-material design options, including: stainless steel clubheads with a titanium face, high-strength aluminum with a titanium clubface, stainless steel with beryllium-copper or brass inserts and more. Moreover, the flurry of new materials continues and the options change every year with new, lightweight, high-strength alloys now leading the trend. Each of these high-profile designs have features and benefits that must be considered and matched with a player's individual abilities and needs. To choose the material and a design that will best optimize distance, accuracy and feel, Golfsmith recommends that you first concentrate on the specifications of the clubhead. The specifications — such as loft, lie and face angle — have a greater influence on ball flight than any differences in materials or design.

Center of Gravity and Effective Loft

CONVENTIONAL SIZE HEAD   LARGER HEAD TITANIUM

CG location

CG location

The further back the center of gravity is in the clubhead, the greater the effective loft (loft at impact).

Diagram 1-2

However, the size of the clubhead can effect trajectory. Usually, the larger the clubhead the higher the trajectory for any given loft. In other words, a large clubhead with a 10-degree loft will hit the ball higher than a small clubhead with a 10-degree loft, everything else being equal. This is due to the location of the center of gravity in the clubhead. Larger clubheads will typically have a center of gravity that is farther back in the clubhead. This can vary, depending on the material of the clubhead. The farther back the center of gravity, the more effective loft (loft at impact) the club will have (see Diagram 1-2). Larger clubheads also can be more forgiving on "off-center" hits. Most of the larger clubhead designs have a hitting surface that is larger than the more conventional size heads. And, on a less technical note, larger heads simply give some players more confidence. The exception to this is the larger head also has a much taller face, which can raise the center of gravity and because there is more material in the face prevents the center of gravity from moving back farther.

As with the irons, the cosmetics of the clubhead are important. You have to like what you are looking at when you address the golf ball. For some reason, a club that appeals to us cosmetically seems easier to hit. So, choose a clubhead with a finish and a head shape that inspires you.

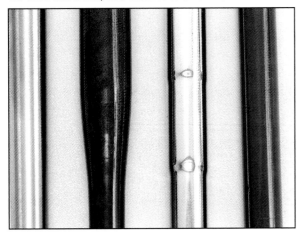
Various Shaft Types

SHAFTS *Golf Club Shafts*

Choosing the right shaft can be one of the most confusing aspects of the club selection process. The weight, flex characteristics and material from which the shaft is constructed and the geometry of the shaft all factor into the feel and overall performance of the golf club.

It also is one of the most important aspects of the club-selection process because shaft weight is a major factor in determining the overall weight of the club. Stainless steel shafts continue to be the most widely used golf club shafts. They can vary in weight from approximately 90 grams – considered ultralight in steel – to the standard-weight steel shaft of 125-130 grams.

The flex designations available in most lines of steel shafts range from ladies' or light flex (very flexible) to senior or "A" flex to men's regular flex to stiff or firm flex to extra-stiff flex. Steel shafts offer a consistency from shaft to shaft not always possible in other shaft materials. Additionally, steel shafts are generally less expensive than more exotic materials, such as composite graphite. However, there are limitations to design specifications in stainless steel shafts that are possible in graphite and other materials.

Graphite, or composite, shafts have become extremely popular, especially in woods, over the last decade. Materials technology enables golf shafts to be constructed using such composite materials with design perimeters that could never be achieved with steel. The weight of graphite composite shafts, for instance, can range from around 40 grams up to 125 grams. Additionally, the range of materials and manufacturing methods available to graphite shafts allows for a broader range of specifications and geometry's to be designed into the shafts. The fact that these options all influence the playing characteristics of the club, a broader range of players can be more easily fit to graphite shafts.

The flex designations available in graphite shafts are the same as in steel shafts. There may be some variation in the terminology, such as using numbers or letters instead of the word designation. However, there are no standards for flex designation in shafts, which means that one shaft company's "R" flex may differ in flex from another company's "R" flex. This is true of both steel and graphite shafts. For this reason, Golfsmith developed the Recommended Swing Speed Range (RSSR) to help customers compare and select shafts, based on the swing speed that optimizes the shaft's performance. Below is a chart to help you select the right shaft flex.

SELECTING THE RIGHT SHAFT FLEX

SHAFT FLEX	DRIVER SWING SPEED	DRIVER CARRY DISTANCE	CLUB FROM 150 YARDS
X - Stiff	105 + mph	260 yards	8- or 9-iron
Stiff	90-105 mph	240 - 260 yards	6- or 7-iron
Regular	80 - 95 mph	210 - 240 yards	5- or 6-iron
Flexible (A flex)	65- 80 mph	180 - 210 yards	4-iron
Ladies (L flex)	under 65 mph	under 180 yards	3-iron/lofted wood

The Golfsmith Clubmaking catalogs list specifications and Recommended Swing Speed Ratings for every shaft offered. Choosing the proper shaft flex is simplified by determining the player's swing speed and the carry distance for particular clubs. Once the specifications of the shaft and the flex are selected, price and cosmetics should be considered.

One of the biggest differences between steel and graphite composite shafts is feel. The feel is influenced by the weight, wall thickness, geometry, stiffness, and bend and balance points of the shaft, as well as the shock-absorbing characteristics of the shaft materials. For instance, graphite is more shock absorbent than steel. There are shock-absorbing options for steel shafts, including inserts that can be incorporated during or after the manufacturing process. According to manufacturers, inserts reduce the low-frequency vibrations at impact.

Not surprisingly, the best way to determine shaft feel is to actually swing the club. There can be real differences in the way a club feels from player to player. If the specifications of the shaft fit the player, there shouldn't be any significant differences in ball flight with different shaft materials. However, the playability, performance and feel differences ultimately are in the eye of the beholder.

With the added flexibility in the design, and the increased costs of materials and manufacturing, graphite-composite shafts are generally more expensive than their steel counterparts. For more information, and a more in depth look at shaft fitting, Golfsmith recommends *The Golfsmith Practical Fitting Program* by Chief Technical Officer Tom Wishon (Stock #8500). It is available in the Golfsmith Clubmaking Catalog.

GRIP SELECTION

One of the most overlooked golf club components is the grip. It should not be. As mentioned before, the grip is the point at which the player connects with the golf club, and therefore, it is key to determining the overall feel of the club. While the grip is a major factor in club feel, it will not have a direct or overwhelming influence on ball flight. The two most important aspects of the grip selection process are size and texture. Grips are offered in a variety of sizes, ranging from junior to men's standard to large to jumbo. Grips are tapered from the butt-end to the mouth (top to bottom), and sizes are determined by measurements at distinctive points along the body of the grip. Most comparative measurements are conducted two inches from the grip cap and six inches from the grip cap. To develop in-between sizes, vary the number of wraps of tape used in the gripping process. Grip size should be determined by hand size, the positioning of the hand and fingers on the grip, and the overall feel of a particular grip size.

Supplies for Gripping

A grip composition, or the materials used to manufacture a grip, has a significant impact on the overall feel of the grip. Grips can feel hard, soft, tacky (sticky), smooth, rough, spongy or textured. When choosing between these various grip textures, consider the weather conditions in which the golfer generally plays (wet or dry climate), the player's perspiration level and any skin sensitivity. In the final analysis, however, "feel" of the material should be the deciding factor. The grip should feel comfortable to the player.

OTHER FACTORS
Swingweight / Total Weight

Swingweight is not the actual weight of the golf club. Swingweight actually refers to the relationship between the weight of the clubhead and the weight of the remainder of the golf club. Swingweight is marked by a letter-number designation for the weight distribution of the golf club, or the balance of the golf club. On the other hand, total weight refers to the actual weight of the entire golf club. The factors that determine the swingweight and total weight of a golf club are club length and the weight of the components. Again, the difference is that swingweight is dictated by the location of the weight on the club, whereas total weight is simply the total weight of the club, regardless of the specific location of the club weighting.

Still, there is no one correct swingweight for all players. The right swingweight provides the player the clubhead feel they want when swinging the golf club. The natural swingweight — the weight of the club components combined with the length of the golf club — generally falls within a range that is acceptable for most players and provides them with good feel. The primary objective is to maintain a consistent swingweight throughout a set of irons. This is obtainable if the clubmaker uses quality parts that are within manufacturer tolerances. Swingweight consistency is also important in woods. However, since traditional-length woods (44-inch drivers, for instance) are no longer the norm, it is not unusual for the swingweight of woods to differ from the swingweight of irons. The key is for the golf club – wood or iron – to have the right clubhead feel for each individual player. This will happen if quality parts that are within manufacturer tolerances are used. Several methods of adjusting swingweight during the assembly process are covered in this book.

The right swingweight provides the player the clubhead feel they want when swinging the golf club.

THE BASICS OF CLUBMAKING

Now that we've laid a foundation with the basics, we now delve more deeply into the proper procedures that enable you to construct world-class golf clubs. We've organized this book in a format that will be easy to follow the first time or to reference later. It is divided into chapters that cover gripping and re-gripping golf clubs, building three different styles of putters, building irons with steel and graphite shafts, and assembling metal woods with steel and graphite shafts. These chapters also include a series of functional clubmaking tips, including: measuring a golf club, trimming steel and graphite shafts, preparing the shafts and the heads for the assembly, and mixing and using the epoxy on each type of club. Detailed photos accompany each section of text to help illustrate the proper clubmaking procedures. Additionally, the Appendix has useful reference material that helps you better understand the craft of clubmaking and all that is involved.

Clubmaking and Fitting Videos

Again, everything you need is outlined in this book. If you have any questions or comments, please contact the Golfsmith Customer Service line at 1-800-925-7709. Customer service representatives are available to help 24-hours-a-day, seven-days-a-week. If you find you are increasingly assembling golf clubs for people other than yourself, we encourage you to read *The Golfsmith Practical Fitting Program*. Golfsmith also has produced a series of instructional clubmaking and fitting videos that provide step-by-step instructions on gripping and re-gripping clubs, shaft fitting and clubfitting, club assembly and re-shafting. When added to this basic assembly book, these resources will give you a complete reference library for basic custom clubmaking and clubfitting.

Before you dive in, here are a few suggestions:

1. Read the entire process of a given task before you actually try to perform it.

2. Lay out all of the tools and components you need before you start. You don't want to get in the middle of a procedure and realize you're missing the materials you need, especially when there is epoxy involved.

3. **ALWAYS WEAR SAFETY GLASSES** when working with epoxies, solvents and machinery. We strongly recommend wearing safety glasses for all procedures in this book.

4. Golfsmith also recommends you use environmentally-friendly and non-flammable solvents when gripping golf clubs.

5. Use hand protection cream or rubber gloves when handling epoxies or solvents.

6. When using any kind of knife or blade, cut away from your body and hands.

7. Always wear gloves, dust masks and safety glasses when working with lead products.

NOTES:

Chapter 2
Gripping & Regripping Golf Clubs

Gripping a golf club (or re-gripping for that matter) is one of the easiest things to do in club assembly or repair. Grips are inexpensive and can really enhance the look and feel of a new club or make an old club feel like new again. If you decide to regrip clubs for friends or as a part of a clubmaking business, you will find it can be one of the most profitable operations you can perform.

Deciding on which type of grip to use can be confusing. There are literally hundreds of options. The basic types of slip-on grips that are available can be classified as rubber composition, rubber composition with half cord or full cord, synthetic rubber and thermoplastic. Wrap-style grips include the old style leather wrap, or more recently, the synthetic rubber wrap-style grips and wrap grips that are actually made of extruded polyurethane. These types of grips are a little more expensive and take a little more time to put on, but many people like their classic look and softer feel.

In deciding what type of grip to choose, consider the composition of the grip, the feel of the material and the look of the grip. The size of the grip can also be important, so if you are unsure on how to determine the right size of grip, refer to chapter one or contact your local clubmaker, golf professional or call Golfsmith for assistance. If possible, and because the feel of the grip is so important in the overall feel of the club, try sampling different materials and compositions to find the one that feels right.

Once you have decided on which grip you want to install, it is time to assess what you will need for installation. Refer to page 26 for a list of tools and supplies required for the task of gripping and/or re-gripping a golf club. The tools, including a rubber vise clamp, a grip stripper and a tape stripper, are good investments because they can be used over and over. A grip-sizing gauge is also handy for checking out the size of the grips once they are installed. Supplies such as grip tape and grip solvent are also needed and cost very little per club to use.

Before getting started, please review all of the pages in this section. We suggest you practice gripping or regripping on a few old clubs before you try this for the first time. Once you have reviewed all of the procedures and performed the operation a couple of times, you should realize how easy it is and how little time the process actually takes. It is really amazing how new grips on old clubs can make those clubs feel and play like new.

Once you master the process of gripping or regripping golf clubs, you will be ready for the next step, assembling a golf club. Chapters 3, 4 and 5 cover all the basics of building metal woods, irons, wedges and putters. We think you will find the process very rewarding, and fun!

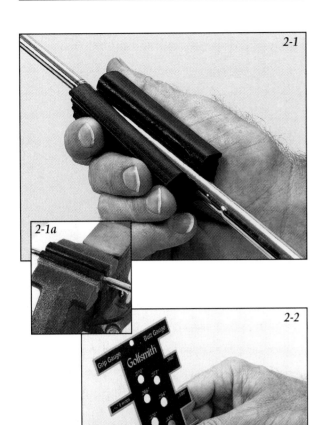

Before you actually begin the process of gripping a golf club, you must take precautions to protect the shaft from damage. The Rubber Vise Clamp (Stock #913) is good for protecting the shaft (graphite or steel) in a vise (see photo 2-1). It allows you to tighten the vise firmly enough to hold the club without damaging the shaft. The clamp simply slips over the center portion of the shaft. Then, place the club in the vise and tighten around the shaft clamp (see photo 2-1a).

Before removing an existing grip, use the All-in-One Gauge (Stock #8989) or calipers to measure the grip (see photo 2-2). You should measure two inches down from the butt cap of the grip. You can also take a second measurement six inches down from the butt cap for a second reference point. Record the size for reference in sizing the new grips.

Removing the old grip can be done using several different types of tools. Photo 2-3 shows the Utility Knife (Stock #853) with the Hooked Blades (Stock #8533). Using this knife, simply place the hook portion of the blade under the mouth of the grip and slice the grip all the way up through the butt. Do not pull the blade towards you. Work it away from you. The blade should cut through most grip materials easily.

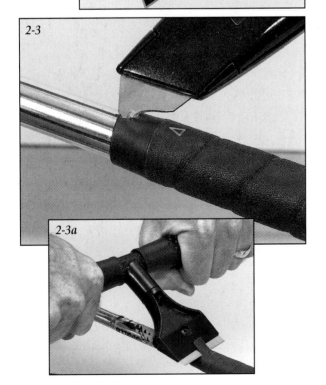

Photo 2- 3a shows the Grip Stripper (Stock #7596). This tool is designed for the task. It keeps both hands occupied for safety and allows you to push away from your body. To remove the grip using this tool, simply start the blade at the mouth of the grip and push it through the butt of the grip. Then, peel the grip off.

Most of the time the tape will not come off with the grip. The old tape must be removed before new tape can be applied. The tape can be removed with a knife or scraper. Remember, always work away from your body. Photo 2-4 shows the Stock #8228 Grip Tape Remover for use with steel or graphite shafts. To remove the tape, start at the end closest to the head, place the curved blade where the tape starts, and push up towards the butt of the shaft. The tape will come off in strips (as shown).

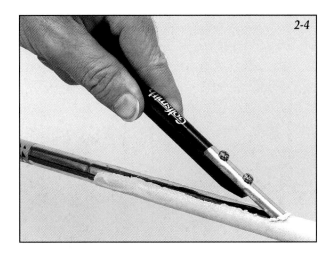

You can rotate the shaft until the majority of the tape is removed. Next, take a cloth damp with grip solvent and wipe down the grip area of the shaft. This removes any tape residue that might still be on the shaft.

After cleaning the butt end of the shaft, place the new grip along side the shaft and note how far down the new grip will go. This prevents putting the tape too far down the shaft (see photo 2-5).

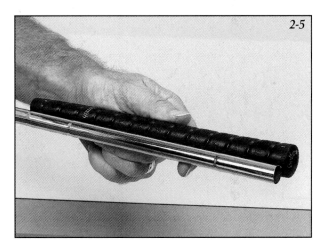

There are two basic sizes of two-sided grip tapes that can be used. One is a ¾ inch that is spiral wrapped around the butt end of the shaft (see photo 2-6). The other is the 2-inch tape that is simply placed on the shaft vertically and then wrapped around (see photo 2-6a). In both cases be sure there is approximately ½ inch hanging over the butt of the shaft. This will be tucked into the butt of the shaft. The 2-inch tape can be placed on top and wrapped around the back (as pictured) or placed underneath the shaft and wrapped around on top. On most shafts, there will be overlap. Try and get the tape as smooth as possible. Once the tape is in place, **Remove the backing on the tape**, exposing the adhesive. Failure to do so will prevent the grip from adhering to the tape and shaft.

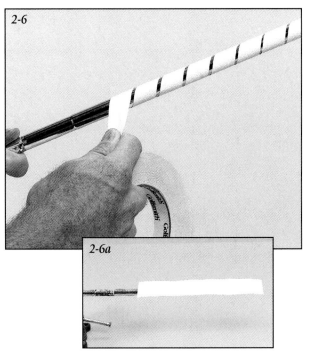

NOTE: The 2-inch tape is a little more economical (more clubs can be done per role) and can be applied with the club in the vise.

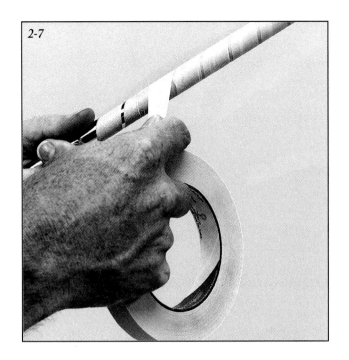

2-7

The ¾-inch tape is applied while holding the club out of the vise. Also, when gripping large butt diameter grips, it is recommended to use ¾-inch gripping tape, wrapped around the shaft.

If a larger grip size is needed, build-up tape (masking tape) can be applied prior to the two-sided tape. Photo 2-7 shows the application of ¾-inch masking tape. The layers of build up need to be overlapped as shown to prevent gaps in the tape. 2-inch masking tape is used when 2-inch two-sided tape is used. When applying 2-inch masking tape, alternate wrapping the tape from front to back with one strip to back to front with the second strip, etc. The sizing chart in the Appendex on page 112 tells how much build-up tape to add for different size grips.

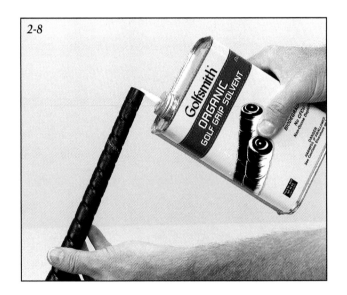

2-8

Plug the hole in the butt end of the grip with your finger (or a golf tee if you prefer) and pour some grip solvent into the mouth of the grip. Do not fill the grip up (see photo 2-8).

Caution! Never use a flammable fluid in grip application.

After pouring some grip solvent into the grip, pinch the mouth of the grip together and turn the grip up and down to coat the inside of the grip with the solvent (see photo 2-9).

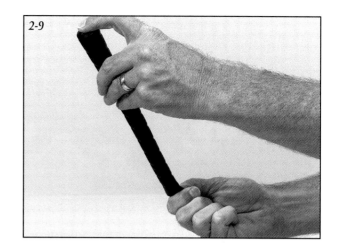

Release you finger or the golf tee plug on the butt end of the shaft and pour the solvent over the grip tape (see photo 2-10). Be sure to coat all of the tape with the solvent. If necessary, pour more solvent from the can on the grip to insure all of the tape is coated.

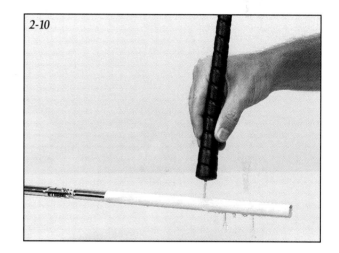

Working quickly but methodically, begin slipping the grip onto the shaft. Hold the grip as shown in photo 2-11 between the grip and forefinger and squeeze slightly to obtain a flared shape. Push the flared mouth up and over the shaft butt.

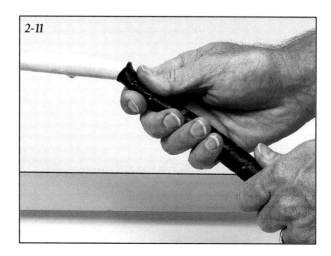

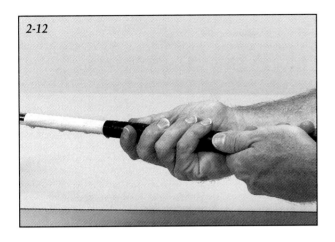

2-12

Once the mouth of the grip is over the butt of the shaft, quickly slide the grip all the way down until you feel the end of the grip hit against the butt of the shaft (see photo 2-12). You can take the club out of the vise and tap the butt of the club lightly on a hard surface (like the floor) to make sure the grip is all the way on or simply push firmly with your palm on the grip cap to insure the grip is all the way on.

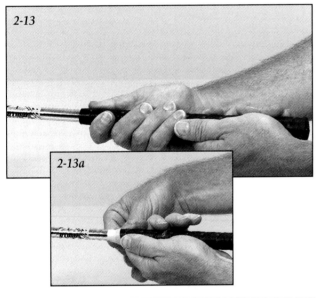

2-13

2-13a

One thing you can do to make a grip a little smaller is stretch it down the shaft (see photo 2-13). This is done by pulling the grip down approximately ½ inch to ¾ inch when it is installed. While holding the grip in the stretched position, tape around the mouth of the grip with masking tape to hold it in the stretched position (see photo 2-13a). After the solvent has dried, remove the tape and the grip will hold it's stretched out position. This makes the grip approximately 1/64-inch undersized. See the sizing chart on page 112.

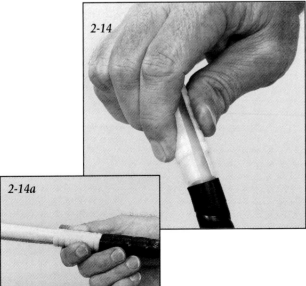

2-14

2-14a

There are grip installation tools that aid in getting the grip on the shaft. The Grip Installation Tool helps prevent grip splitting during installation. To use, simply place the armature in the mouth of the grip (see photo 2-14).

Once the solvent has been applied to the grip tape, slide the entire tool and grip assembly onto the shaft. The tool then slides down towards the shaft tip and is removed (see photo 2-14a).

The Stock #1819 Grip Installer Tool is designed to be used when installing grips on shafts with oversize butt diameters. It is recommended for use when installing grips on .865" or .700" butt shafts, and sizes in between. It also works well on conventional butt shafts and grips. To use, slip a lubricated grip onto the tool as shown in photo 2-15.

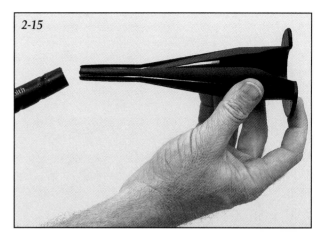

NOTE: When gripping large butt diameter grips, it is recommended to use ¾-inch gripping tape, wrapped around the shaft.

Working quickly, slip the whole assembly over the shaft butt (see photo 2-15a). The tool then slides down, expanding the mouth of the grip over the butt of the shaft.

Once the grip mouth is over the butt and the grip is sliding down the shaft the tool can be removed by pulling it down and to the side as shown (see photo 2-15b). Once the tool is removed, push the grip all the way on (see photo 2-15c). Again, be sure the butt of the shaft is all the way up against the inside butt of the grip. A reminder, use plenty of grip solvent and work quickly, but don't rush. Rushing causes mistakes.

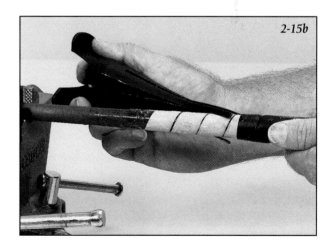

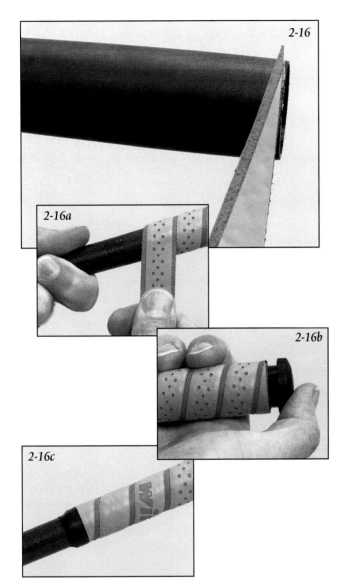

2-16

2-16a

2-16b

2-16c

Another popular grip for the large butt diameter shafts is the wrap-style, like the Winn wrap. These grips are sold as a strip of material and are wrapped around the shaft. Many grips have an adhesive backing that sticks right on the shaft, so no grip tape is needed. To install this type of grip, first peel off the backing strip to expose the adhesive backing. The butt end on most of these grips is the end farthest from the logo. Start the grip, as shown in photo 2-16, and wrap it around the tip of the shaft using firm pressure.

Most of the wrap-style models are now designed to overlap (see photo 2-16a), like leather grips. After wrapping the grip two to three times around the shaft, hold the grip firmly and install the end cap into the butt of the shaft (see photo 2-16b). Press the cap all the way into the butt of the shaft so the edges of the cap cover the top edge of the shaft and grip. This is important because the cap will overlap and lock the top wrap of the grip to the shaft. Once the grip is installed, finish wrapping the grip to its end.

Most of these grips are sold with a strip of shiny black tape. This strip is wrapped around the end of the grip to secure it to the shaft (see photo 2-16c).

Removing Grips

There is a way to remove grips on clubs without cutting them off. The Blade-Style Grip Remover (Stock #8215) enables you to remove a grip with minimal effort and preserve it for re-installation. The first step is to pour grip solvent over the blade portion of the remover as shown in photo 2-17.

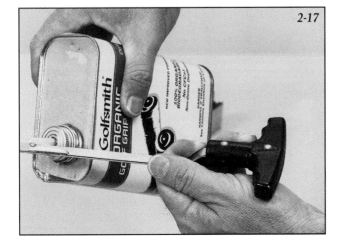

2-17

Work the blade under the mouth of the grip (see photo 2-18). The tool will slide up into the grip to the butt end of the club. Work the tool quickly around the circumference of the shaft. It may be necessary to add a little more grip solvent.

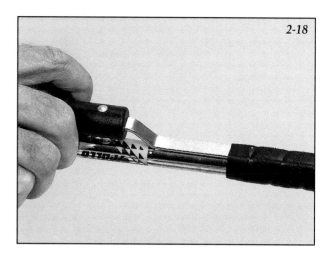

2-18

Once the tool has been worked around the circumference of the shaft, both the grip and the tool should slide off the shaft easily (see photo 2-19).

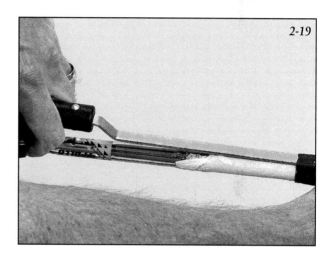

2-19

List of Supplies Needed for Gripping and Regripping:

- ❑ Golf Grips

- ❑ ¾-inch (Stock #902A or #9025) or 2-inch (Stock #902B or #9026) two-sided tape

- ❑ Flame Resistant grip solvent (Stock #9158 or #916A)

- ❑ Blade-Style Grip Remover (Hooked Blades-Stock #8533)
  with Utility Knife- Stock #853 or Straight Blade Grip Stripper- Stock #8533)

- ❑ ¾-inch or 2-inch masking tape – (used only for build up tape when creating oversize grips) - *optional*

- ❑ Rubber Vise Clamp (Stock #913) – *optional only if vise is not used*

- ❑ All-In-One-Gauge (Stock #8989) or calipers – *optional*

- ❑ Tape Stripper (Stock #8228 Grip Tape Remover for use on graphite and steel shafts, – *optional*

- ❑ Grip Sizer (Stock #937) – *optional*

- ❑ Grip Installation Tool (Stock #1819) – *optional*

- ❑ Grip Installation Tool for big butt shafts (Stock #1819) – *optional, but highly recommended for use with big butt shafts and grip.*

Chapter 3
Metal Wood Assembly

Metal woods came on the modern scene in the early 1970s, but wood-shaped heads made from metal material were actually produced as early as the 1890s. They did not dominate then because there was no real performance advantage, other than possibly durability, in using these aluminum heads over the wood heads of the time. Today, "Metal Woods" dominate the market. There are actually players on the PGA Tour today that have never played with a wooden wood.

There are several reasons why the metal wood has come to dominate the golfing world. The most significant reason is the fact that the new generation of metal woods made of stainless steel, titanium, high-strength aluminum and combinations of these and other metals do offer players some performance advantages over the persimmons and laminated maple heads of the not-to-distant past. Metal casting processes for golf clubs developed in the late 1960s and early 1970s have evolved to produce stainless metal woods that are more forgiving on off-center hits due to the perimeter weighting feature inherent in most metal wood designs. With even lighter materials such as titanium and aluminum being common in today's metal woods, larger heads that are not heavier are being produced, which increase the effect of perimeter weighting. These facts, and the fact that almost all of the best players in the world now play metal woods (not to mention all the marketing dollars spent), drive the overwhelming dominance of metal woods today. We have not even included assembly of wooden woods in this text because, frankly, with the exception of some die-hard traditionalist, there is no call for it any more.

From an assembly standpoint, metal woods can be much easier to put together than the old persimmon and laminated wooden woods. This chapter will cover the proper assembly techniques for metal woods using both steel and graphite shafts. Golfsmith carries a number of metal woods manufactured from various stainless steels, titanium, aluminum and combinations of these materials. Also, Golfsmith was the first to produce a head manufactured from MMC (Metal Matrix Composite) material. This is an aluminum and ceramic composite that is lighter and stronger than titanium.

The initial step in making a metal wood is selecting the components you would like to assemble. We have mentioned heads, but the shaft selection and the grip selection are just as important to the overall performance of the club. Chapter one of this book and the Golfsmith Component Catalog helps guide you through the process of selecting the right shaft and grip to fit your game. Golfsmith has a staff of professionally trained people to help you during the selection and assembly process. Either through our retail locations or our toll-free 24-hour-a-day service line, you get the answers to your club selection and assembly questions.

Once you have made the selection, please study the assembly process thoroughly. The step-by-step procedures are designed to guide you in a simple, chronological process, the result being a professionally assembled golf club. If you have already assembled other types of clubs, these steps will probably be easier to understand.

Supplies Needed for Assembly of Metal Woods.

Nevertheless, be sure to take plenty of time to follow and finish each step completely.

Golfsmith prides itself on being a leader in the development of high-end components, which offer the latest in technology. Using Golfsmith components and the instructions outlined in this chapter, you can assemble and play with clubs that reflect the latest in golf club technology.

METAL WOOD ASSEMBLY WITH A STEEL SHAFT

Shaft preparation and assembly

Once you have selected the shaft, you must trim for the proper flex and club number of the head you want to assemble. All parallel tip steel shafts come with recommended shaft trimming instructions to tell you how much to trim from the tip and the butt of the shaft. Follow these trimming instructions precisely if you want the club to play as intended by the manufacturer. As the photo to the left shows, you must first mark the tip of the shaft and cut for flex. Lay the shaft down on a club ruler and, following the trimming instructions, mark the amount to be trimmed from the tip with a marker (see photo 3-1).

There are several ways to cut a steel shaft. Photo 3-2 shows the use of the Super Shaft Cutter (Stock #858). To use this cutter, simply loosen the knob and place it over the shaft tip, aligning the blade directly on the line marking the spot of the cut. Gently tighten the cutting tool by turning the knob. Once the blade is tight on the shaft, begin rotating the blade around the shaft. If the blade slides off the mark, re-position and tighten. After rotating the cutting tool around the shaft a few times, tighten the knob tighter. Continue to rotate the blade, tightening after several rotations. When the cut is complete, the shaft tip should break off clean at the intended cut line. There may be small burrs created from the cut. If so, use a medium or fine hand cutting file or sand paper to remove or debur these edges. An alternative method (see photo 3-2a) is to use a cutoff wheel (Stock #8581), which attaches to a bench grinder or electronic motor (minimum ⅓ hp motor). This wheel is designed to cut steel or graphite shafts quickly and efficiently. **Be sure to wear protective eyewear when you use power equipment.**

Once the shaft is cut, the shaft tip must be abraded. This "roughing up" of the surface helps insure the bond of the shaft, epoxy and head. Before this is done, note the bore depth of the hosel of the clubhead. You determine this by taking a pencil or something similar and putting it into the hosel. Mark the depth then pull the pencil out, lay it next to the shaft and mark the shaft. This will tell you the depth the shaft must go into the head. You must be sure the shaft is going to the bottom of the bore. Be careful not to rough up the shaft beyond where the shaft will penetrate the hosel of the club. Next, take coarse grit sandpaper and cut it into approximately a one-inch wide by five- or six-inch long strip. Place the shaft in a vise (use protective shaft clamp Stock #8288 or Rubber Vise Clamp Stock #913) and secure. If the head is a style that requires a ferrule, you can abrade slightly above the hosel line. As shown in photo 3-3, place the strip over the tip of the shaft and work the sandpaper back and forth. You will need to rotate the shaft so that all sides of the tip are abraded. Once the shaft tip is completely abraded, clean the tip with a damp cloth.

3-2a

3-3

SPECIAL NOTE:
On heads with the hosel weight port, the total bore depth is deeper than the shafting bore depth. The shaft should only go to the top of the hosel weight port. These areas are separated by a ledge (see Diagram 3-1 below) preventing the shaft from going too deep. When premeasuring for shaft depth, only measure to the ledge.

Diagram 3-1

Proper Shafting Depth

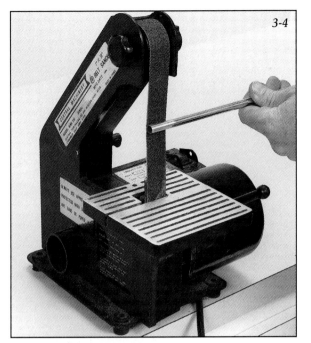

3-4

An alternative method is to use a 30-inch (pictured) or a 42-inch belt sander. A medium or coarse belt can also be used. Because the belt is moving very fast, this technique requires you to rotate the shaft quickly while applying a moderate amount of pressure to the belt (see photo 3-4). If you have not used this method before, we recommend you practice on several old shafts before attempting it on the one for use in your club. Although this is a quicker and more efficient method, it does require some skill and technique. As always when using power equipment, be sure to wear protective eyewear. A medium to fine metal file can also be used to rough up the tip of a steel shaft (see photo 3-4a). See photo 3-4b for a final look.

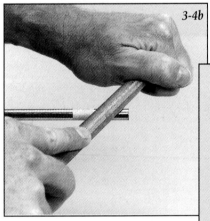

3-4b

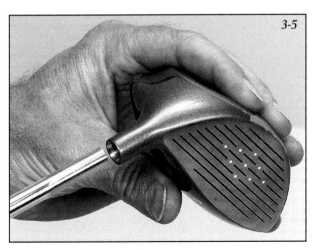

3-4a

After cutting and abrading the tip of the shaft, test fit the shaft into the hosel. (see photo 3-5) It is very important to make sure the shaft goes all the way to the bottom of the bore. The proper bore depth should still be noted on the shaft. If not, repeat the process described earlier on page 29.

3-5

If the head requires a ferrule, it can be installed onto the shaft prior to epoxying the head in place or at the time the head is installed. To install the ferrule without epoxy, first place the ferrule over the tip of the shaft. One handy tool you can use to install the ferrule is the Mr. T Ferrule installer (Stock #8690).

To use, simply place the ferrule on the tip of the shaft as in photo 3-6. Place the tool over the ferrule and press firmly down (see photo 3-6a). The ferrule is then set approximately one inch onto the shaft (see photo 3-6b). Once this is done, then use the hosel of the clubhead to drive the ferrule down the shaft tip to the exact full penetration depth (see photo 3-7).

Another ferrule installation tool you can use is the Stock #351 Ferrule Installation Tool. To use, check the bore depth with the knurled rod (see photo 3-6c) and then set the rod in place by tightening the round handle. Next, turn the tool around, and with a light tapping motion, tap the ferrule onto the shaft (see photo 3-6d). This puts the ferrule at the precise point of full hosel penetration. When using heads with the hosel weight port you must not let the knurled rod go to the bottom of the hosel weight port. This will result in the ferrule being installed too far up the shaft. The knurled rod must go only to the bottom of the shaft bore. There is an edge or lip indicating the bottom of the hosel bore and the start of the weight port. By running the knurled rod down the inside edge of the hosel, you should be able to set the knurled rod at the proper depth on the bottom edge of the shaft bore portion of the hosel bore. (see diagram 3-1, page 29)

As mentioned earlier, the clubhead can actually be used to install the ferrule to its full penetration. Once the ferrule has been partially installed, simply take the head and use it as the driving tool to put the ferrule in exactly the right place. Holding the shaft firmly in one hand and the head in the other (see photo 3-7), firmly tap the butt of the shaft on a hard surface. This will drive the shaft through the ferrule and to the bottom of the bore.

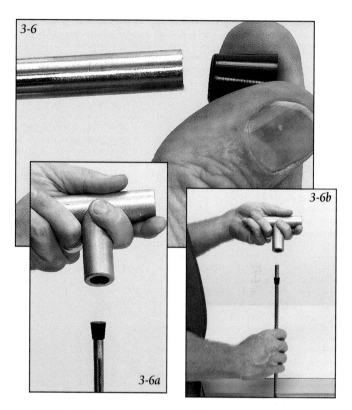

3-6

3-6b

3-6a

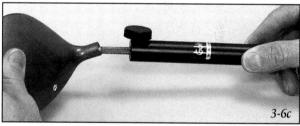

3-6c

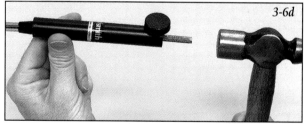

3-6d

3-7

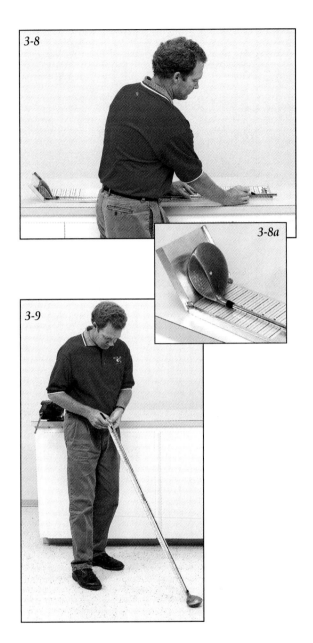

3-8

3-8a

3-9

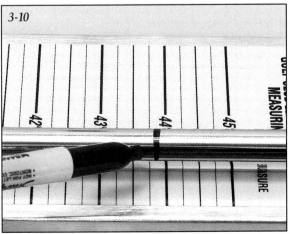

3-10

NOTE: An alternative method is to install the ferrule at the time the head is being epoxied to the shaft. To do this, simply dip the tip of the shaft into the epoxy mix. Slide the ferrule over the shaft tip.

You can then drive the ferrule on with the head as shown in photo 3-7. The head should then be removed and the proper amount of epoxy should be applied to the shaft tip and the hosel of the head. That will be discussed later in this chapter. See photo 3-18 and 3-19 on page 35 and 36 for reference.

Photo 3-8 shows measuring the shaft for cutting to final length. With the shaft fully inserted on the head, measure the club for final length.

SPECIAL CAUTION! *Do not force the head onto the shaft. A mechanical bond could be created, making it difficult to remove the head. If the head gets stuck on the shaft, put the shaft in a vice and gently twist the head off. If you cannot twist the head off, it will be necessary to use a 48-inch Ram Rod to get the head off. Place the rod down the shaft from the butt end of the shaft until it stops. Gently tap the end of the rod with a hammer. This should drive the head off the shaft. The True Measure Precision Club Rule (Stock #4606) works well on your bench or tabletop. It has a hinged flange that allows the club to sole properly when measuring the length of the club (see photo 3-8a inset).*

The 48-inch Combination Ruler is used by putting the club in playing position and marking the shaft for the length cut (see photo 3-9). Whether using the 48-inch Club Ruler or the True Measure Club Rule, it is important to mark the shaft properly for the final length cut. Photo 3-10 shows a close up of the mark indicating where the shaft is to be cut for final length. Note the mark is approximately ⅛ inch shorter than the intended final length. In this example the final club length is to be 44 inches. It is recommended to allow for at least ⅛ inch to ¼ inch for the tip of the grip cap. See photo 3-37 on page 42 to see the assembled measurement and how it should look.

The shaft butt can now be cut for the final length of the club. The methods for cutting the butt of the shaft are the same as for cutting the tip of the shaft (see photo 3-11). You can use the Super Shaft Cutter (Stock #858) with the shaft in a vise (see inset 3-11a) or the 6-inch Cutoff Wheel (Stock #8581) on a bench grinder (see inset 3-11b). Be sure to cut as precisely as possible. Check for burrs left from the cut and if necessary deburr the edges with a medium or fine cutting hand file or sandpaper.

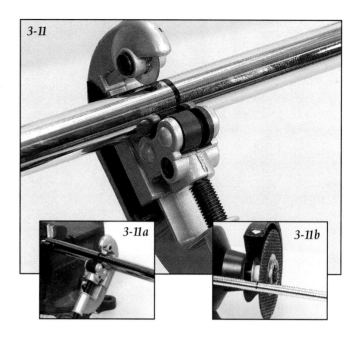

After cutting, check the length again. Note in photo 3-12 that the cut shaft is approximately ⅛ inch below the desired final club length.

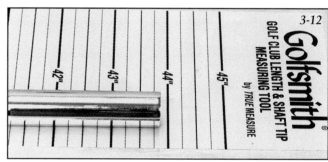

The final step before the actual assembly process begins is to check to see what the swingweight of the club will be. To do this, you will need an old grip that is split. The grip should be the same kind that will be used in the final assembly process, or at least one that is the same weight as the grip that will be used in the final assembly. This easily slips over the butt of the shaft. The purpose is to simulate what the final swingweight will be after assembly and to determine if any weight will need to be added during the assembly process. The head should be placed on the tip end of the shaft dry (with no epoxy), making sure the shaft goes in the head to the bottom of the bore. Since the ferrule is pre-set, you can tell when the head is on properly. Now, check the swingweight reading (see photo 3-13 and 13a). In this example, observe that the swingweight is approximately C9.

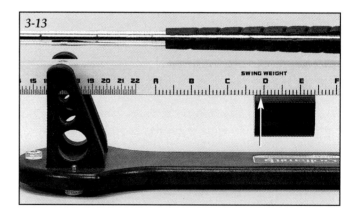

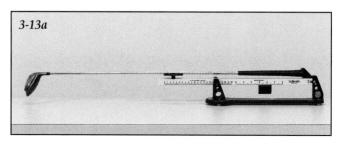

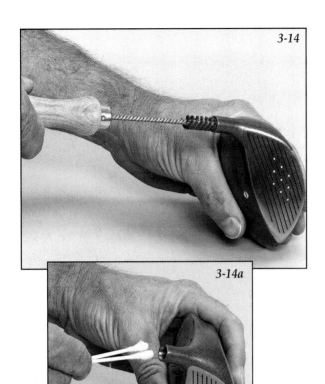

3-14

3-14a

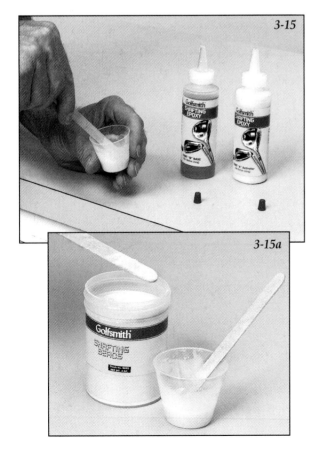

3-15

3-15a

NOTE: Measuring the swingweight of a golf club prior to and after assembly is not required in the assembly process. For a definition of swingweight and its function, refer to the Appendix and the Glossary of clubmaking terms.

Golfsmith sells several models of swingweight scales. There are several models of swingweight scales in the Golfsmith Components Catalog that will work.

Before you can epoxy the shaft into the head, you must clean out the hosel. This is necessary to clean out any dirt, oil, etc. that may have been left in the hosel during the manufacturing process. The first recommended step is to use a Hosel Cleaning Brush (Stock #8625). As illustrated in photo 3-14, the silicon carbide bristles on the Flex Hone Tool are pushed into the hosel with a twisting motion. This will remove or loosen unwanted material in the hosel. It also roughs up the inside of the hosel, which aids in the adhesion process. The next step is to take some cotton swabs (see photo 3-14a), dip them into acetone and swab out the hosel. This will clean out the entire remaining residue. Once you have swabbed out the hosel with acetone, set it aside to dry for a few minutes.

NOTE: This is a very important step. Many epoxy bond failures are due to contaminants in the epoxy that come from the hosel.

It's time to epoxy the head onto the shaft. We recommend using the Golfsmith Shafting Epoxy (Stock #9095 for half-pint quantity). Parts A and B mix at a 1 : 1 ratio. It is best to use mixing cups similar to the one pictured. Simply pour out equal amounts of Part A and Part B in separate cups, then mix together. It is very important to mix thoroughly. Mix for at least 1 minute . Mix until the epoxy is a consistent color throughout (see photo 3-15). Photo inset 3-15a shows a product called epoxy beads. They are tiny glass beads that can be added to epoxy to insure adequate epoxy cushion between the shaft and hosel wall. These beads can eliminate the possibility of shafting a club off-center. If the shaft is a loose fit in the hosel, we recommend using these beads (Stock #9082). If the shaft is a good fit and does not lean when put into the hosel, the beads are not necessary.

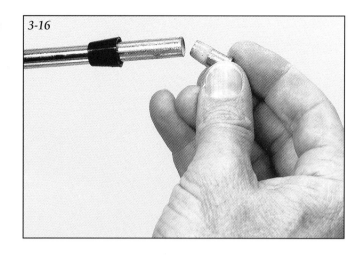

3-16

If weight needs to be added for swingweighting purposes, there are several methods of doing this. Photo 3-16 shows a shaft tip weight being installed in the tip of the shaft. They are available in various weights in the Golfsmith catalog. If using these type of weights, simply coat the inside of the shaft tip with a small amount of epoxy, dip the weight in the epoxy and insert the weight into the tip of the shaft.

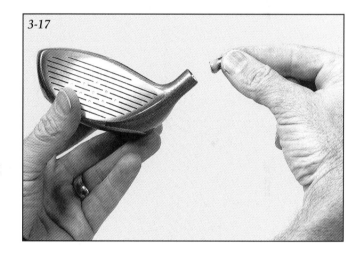

3-17

Many of the heads in the Golfsmith Components Catalog are designed with a hosel weight port, which allows a special lead or tungsten weight plug to be installed into the bottom of the hosel. As with the shaft tip weights, this allows for increasing the swingweight at the time of assembly. To install, simply coat the weight in epoxy and drop in the hosel (see photo 3-17). Be sure the weight falls all the way to the bottom of the weight port (see Diagram 3-2).

Diagram 3-2
Proper Position of Hosel Bore Weight in Head.

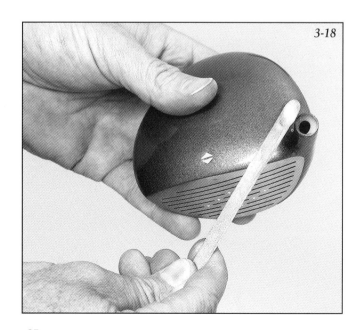

3-18

It's time to install the shaft. Using a mixing stick, put a small bead of epoxy on the inside of the hosel (see photo 3-18). Do not fill the hosel. A small amount is all that is necessary.

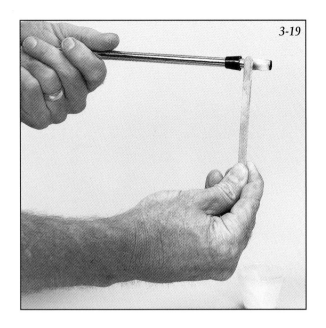

3-19

Next, take the mixing stick and coat the outside of the tip of the shaft with epoxy (see photo 3-19). Be sure to get good coverage over the tip of the shaft.

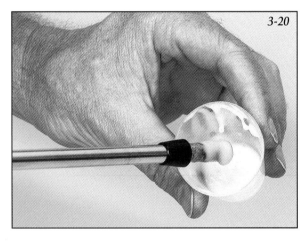

3-20

One option, instead of using the mixing stick, is to simply dip the shaft tip into the epoxy mix as shown in photo 3-20. Again, be sure you get good coverage on the outside of the shaft tip.

Once you have dipped the shaft tip in the epoxy, you can use it to spread the bead on the inside of the hosel (see photo 3-21).

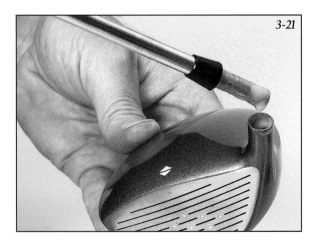

3-21

Install the shaft by inserting it into the hosel, slowly rotating or twisting the shaft as it goes into the hosel (see photo 3-22). Once you have the shaft all the way in the hosel, pull the shaft about half way out, still rotating it, and re-insert the shaft all the way. This insures that epoxy is covering every area inside the hosel and on the shaft tip.

Turn the club upside down and gently tap the butt of the shaft on a hard surface (see photo 3-23). Do not tap on vinyl or wood floor surfaces. This helps insure the shaft is inserted all the way to the bottom of the hosel.

3-22

Using a paper towel dampened with solvent, wipe the excess epoxy off of the hosel and ferrule area (see page 37, photo 3-24). It is much easier to wipe this area clean when the epoxy is still wet, so be meticulous. Get it as clean as possible. Set the club upright, as shown in photo 3-24a, for curing. The Golfsmith epoxy, Stock #9095, is a 24-hour cure epoxy. Although the epoxies actual gel time may be shorter, it is not recommended that the club be used for at least 24 hours. The epoxy mix that is not used should be left out in the mixing cup. It will be your reference to see if the epoxy has cured.

3-23

After the appropriate time for curing has past (approximately 24 hours), check the mixing cup to see if the mix used for the club has cured (see photo 3-25). If the epoxy in the cup appears soft and not cured, do not hit the club. Cure rates can vary depending on the outside temperature. At room temperature, 24 hours should be sufficient. The Golfsmith 24 hour epoxy will be very hard when it cures. If the epoxy is cured correctly, it should appear hard and if pressed firmly with a mixing stick, should leave little, if any indentation.

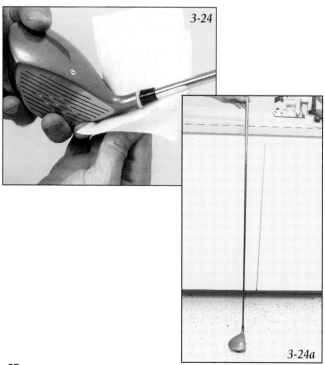

3-24

3-24a

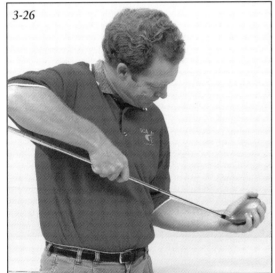

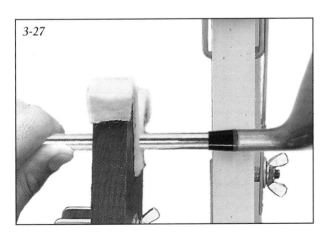

SPECIAL NOTE: Outside temperatures can effect the curing time. The warmer it is, the faster and harder the epoxy cures. It is still recommended no club be used for a minimum of 24 hours after assembly. Check the head for tightness (see photo 3-26).

If the club you have assembled has a ferrule, the ferrule portion of the club may need finishing or cleaning up after the assembly is complete. Most ferrules will be slightly larger than outside diameter of the hosel. To get a clean, professional look, it is recommended that the ferrule be "turned down" or smoothed so it is the same diameter of the hosel. A linen polishing belt on a 30 inch or 42 inch belt sander can be used (see photo 3-27. Pictured is a close up of the Stock #8209 ferrule turning support arm and the Stock #446 42 inch belt sander with motor). You must be very careful not to damage the finish of the clubhead. Also, applying too much pressure to the ferrule can cause damage to the ferrule. If a belt sander is not available, the ferrule can be turned down by hand. Use masking tape to cover the shaft and hosel. Sand the ferrule down using a file and a fine grit sand paper.

If you use a 30-inch or 40-inch belt sander, we recommend you practice on a few old clubs before you start. If the ferrule is almost flush with the hosel, you can skip this procedure and simply go to applying acetone to the ferrule with a cotton swab or paper towel. This will give the ferrule a nice, professional shine (see photo 3-27a).

One method of fine tuning the swingweight of the club after the head is assembled is to add weight down the shaft using lead powder. This should not be done in addition to using hosel weights or shaft tip weights.

NOTE: SensiCore is a dampening core inside some steel or graphite shafts that reduces uncomfortable vibration from shots hit off the sweet spot. Because this core is inserted into the inside of the shaft, clubs made with these shafts cannot have the swingweight adjusted by inserting lead powder or other weight through the butt end of the shaft. The SensiCore insert will not allow the passage of these materials nor will it allow a Ram Rod or Long Hot Rod through the shaft.

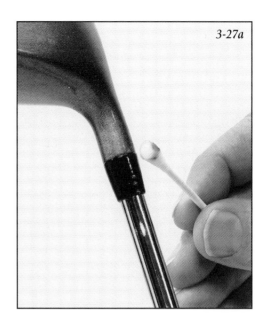

3-27a

Before you actually add the lead, you must check the swingweight of the club without the grip on (see photo 3-28). Swingweight readings without a grip on the club will be approximately 10 swingweight points higher than the actual final swingweight. For example, the photo shows the swingweight of this club to be D9 without the grip. If we did nothing but put a standard rubber grip on without adding any weight, the final swingweight of this club would be around C9.

To increase the swingweight using tungsten powder (Stock #9466), simply pour the lead powder into the butt end of the shaft (see photo 3-29). It will flow down to the tip end, or head end of the club. You can pre-measure the powder in a mixing cup and weigh it on a scale to predetermine how much weight you are adding. Two grams is equivalent to one swingweight point. It is not recommended that more than eight to ten grams of weight be added using this method. More than this amount could effect the playability of the club. Once you have poured the powder into the hosel, gently tap the club against a hard surface with the head end on the ground to ensure the powder goes all the way to the tip of the shaft.

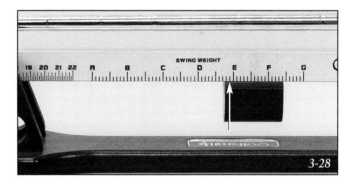

3-28

After adding the powder, set the club back on the swingweight scale to check the weight. In this example, two swingweights were added (four grams). The scale now reads E1, which, when the grip is installed, will give a final swingweight reading of approximately D1 (see photo 3-30).

3-29

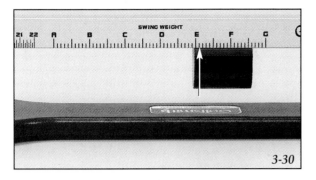

3-30

Once the desired amount of weight is added, a cork must be epoxied down the shaft to prevent the lead powder from coming out (see photo 3-31). There are different types for corks for different types of shafts. Steel wood shafts require Stock #882A cork in the Golfsmith Component Catalog. As shown in photo 3-31, take standard shafting epoxy and, using a mixing stick, apply the epoxy to the cork and drop it into the shaft.

3-31

Using a 45 inch Ram Rod (Stock #864), push the cork down the shaft as far as it will go. Do not jam the rod in as hard as you can. Use a smooth firm pressure to get the cork to the bottom or tip of the shaft, then a couple of firm taps should do. This will set the cork in the proper place (see photo 3-32).

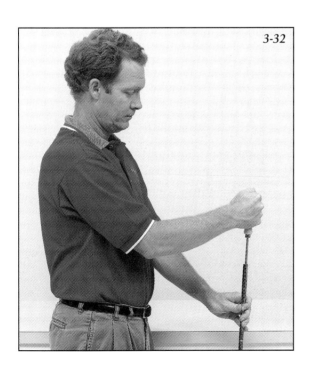

3-32

There will usually be some lead powder that remains loose in the shaft after the cork is installed. You want to remove this from the shaft. Simply turn the shaft but down and tap firmly on a hard surface. The powder residue should all come out the butt of the shaft (see photo 3-33).

3-33

It is important to be sure the cork is as far down the shaft as possible. To do this, place the Ram Rod down the shaft until it stops. Using your thumb (you can mark the rod with a marker), mark the depth of the rod. This is easiest to do if the club is placed in a vice as shown in photo 3-34.

3-34

Remove the rod from the shaft and place it along side the shaft, noting the point you have marked as being the depth of the cork (see photo 3-35). The rod should indicate the powder and cork is at least down to the top of the hosel, and preferably as low into the head as possible. This will vary, depending on how much weight is added. If the rod stops well above the ferrule, it is likely that the cork did not get all the way down into the proper position. If this occurs, take the rod and attempt to ram the cork further down the shaft, then repeat procedures as shown in photos 3-34 and 3-35.

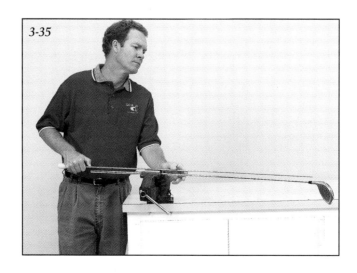

3-35

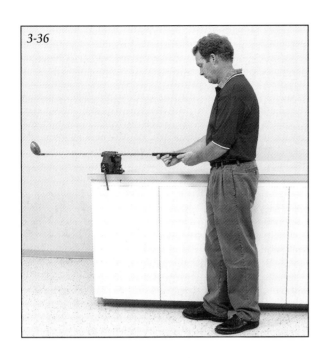

Install the grip (photo 3-36).

NOTE: *For complete gripping instructions, see Chapter 2.*

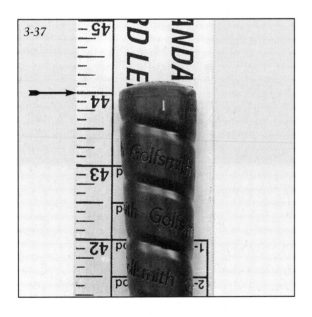

Re-check the length. The length of the club is read from the top of the grip cap, not the crown of the grip (see photo 3-37 with indicator arrow).

Re-check swingweight after assembly.

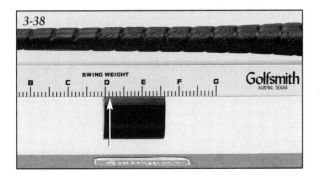

NOTE: *the swingweight in photo 3-38 is approximately D1.*

METAL WOOD ASSEMBLY WITH GRAPHITE SHAFTS

Graphite shafts have seen a resurgence in popularity since the early 1980's. Graphite shafts produced a decade earlier lacked the torsional stability to be effective and went away as fast as they came. Since the early 80s, graphite has seen a steady increase in usage, especially in woods. Today, a high percentage of all woods are sold with graphite shafts. The reason: Graphite offers a wider range in weight than steel, and offers a wide range of playing characteristics with an inherent shock absorbing feature in the actual carbon fiber material that the shafts are made of. The ability to make longer, lighter golf clubs, specifically drivers and fairway woods, is largely possible because of the technological advances made in the materials used in graphite shafts and the manufacturing processes themselves.

Many people new to golf club assembly will shy away from graphite because they think it is more difficult to work with. It really is not. By taking a few extra precautions, working with graphite is just as easy as working with steel. Golfsmith offers literally hundreds of options in graphite. Once you have followed the basic shaft fitting procedures outlined in Chapter 1 and selected a graphite shaft, simply follow the step by step procedures outlined here. The result will be a custom-fit, custom-built metal wood that will give you enjoyment for many rounds to come. A reminder, even if you have assembled clubs with graphite shafts before, follow these steps exactly. Take plenty of time and read through the instructions before you start. If you have any questions, contact a Golfsmith representative at any of our retail locations or call Golfsmith Customer Service (1-800-925-7709) toll-free 24 hours a day, seven days a week.

Today, a high percentage of all woods are sold with graphite shafts.

3-39

Once you have selected the shaft you will use, you must trim it according to the manufacturers recommended trimming instructions. These trimming instructions come with the shaft. Some graphite shafts require the tip of the shaft be trimmed prior to assembly. For this example, the tip will be trimmed. Place the shaft on a club rule and mark the shaft tip for trimming (according to the manufacturers recommended trimming instructions) with a marker (see photo 3-39).

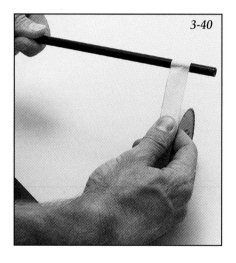
3-40

Once you have marked the shaft for tip trimming, you should tape the shaft just above and up to the intended cut mark with masking tape (see photo 3-40). This helps prevent the graphite fibers from splintering when the shaft is being cut. You can tape the tip of the shaft first, then mark the shaft on the tape itself.

There are, as with steel, several methods of cutting graphite.

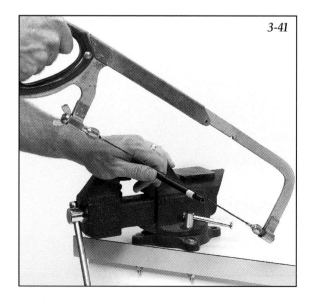
3-41

NOTE: DO NOT USE the Stock #858 Shaft Cutter. It is designed for steel shafts only. Photo 3-41 shows the Stock #8586 Rod Saw Blade. When attached to a standard hack saw this blade cuts graphite cleanly and quickly. Place the shaft in a vice. It is recommended to use the Stock #8288 Pro Metal Vise Clamp to protect the shaft in the vise. To cut the shaft, place the blade on the mark and using a normal sawing motion, cut the tip of the shaft (see photo 3-41). An alternative blade to use is the Stock #8587 Grit–Edge Saw Blade.

An alternative to using the hacksaw is the Cutoff Wheel (Stock #8581). This wheel attaches to a bench grinder or electric motor and cuts graphite, as well as steel. This wheel should be used with at least ⅓ h.p. motors. Photo 3-42 shows the positioning of the shaft when cutting. Simply place the shaft against the wheel and apply slight pressure. The blade will cut the shaft quickly and evenly. As always, be sure to wear safety glasses when using any kind of power equipment.

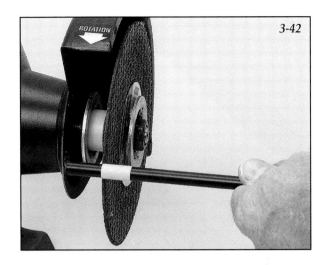

3-42

After trimming the tip of the shaft, you must prepare the tip surface for insertion into the head. Some graphite shafts are painted all the way to the tip of the shaft and others have approximately one inch of the tip unfinished from the factory. In both cases you still have to rough up the surface of the tip. Be sure you know what the bore depth of the head will be before you begin prepping the tip. Measure the bore depth of the hosel with a pencil or similar object and mark the shaft accordingly. See the *SPECIAL NOTE:* on page 29 for important details of this procedure. You may want to tape off the shaft just above the area to be prepped (see photo 3-43). Photo 3-43a shows one technique for prepping the tip of the shaft. A knife can be used for scraping the tip of the shaft. You only want to rough up the amount of the tip that will be in the hosel. Using the knife, position as shown and lightly scrape the tip.

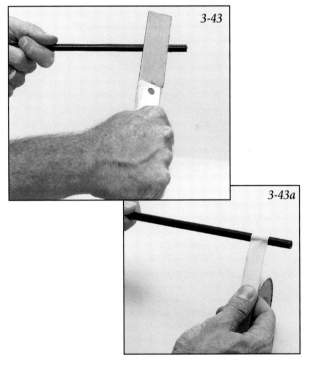

3-43

3-43a

3-43b

3-44

You just want to remove the finish from the tip, or lightly scrape the tip of the shaft on those that do not have the finish on them (see photo 3-44 for view of tip after scraping). DO NOT cut into the fibers of the graphite. You can also use Surface Conditioning Strips (Stock #4875). These strips are used much like sandpaper strips on steel shafts. Simply place the shaft in a vise using a Rubber Vice Clamp (Stock #8249 is recommended). Work the conditioning strip back and forth, being sure to cover the entire circumference of the shaft tip (see page 45, photo 3-43b). Again, it is recommended to tape the shaft above the area to be prepped.

3-44a

The prepped shaft tip using the conditioning strips should look like photo 3-44a when you are finished. After preparing the tip, wipe it off with a clean damp cloth to remove any dust left on the tip. As with steel shafts, this method does require some practice. DO NOT sand into the fibers of the graphite shaft. We recommend you practice on old shafts before attempting on your new shaft.

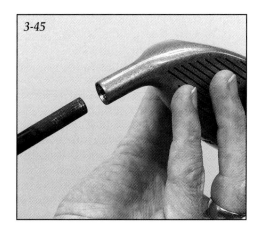

3-45

After preparing the tip of the shaft, test fit the shaft into the hosel of the club you are shafting (see photo 3-45). It is very important that you know the bore depth of the head you are shafting. This will insure that the shaft is going into the head all the way to the bottom of the bore.

If the head requires a ferrule, place the ferrule on to the shaft. The ferrule can be installed onto the shaft prior to epoxying the head in place or at the time the head is installed. To install the ferrule without epoxy, first place the ferrule over the tip of the shaft (see photo 3-46). A tool you can use to help with the installation of ferrules is the Mr. T Ferrule Installer (Stock #8690). After placing the ferrule over the tip of the shaft, use the installer to drive the ferrule on, approximately one-inch onto the shaft (see photos 3-47 and 3-47a). The ferrule will be driven the remainder of the way on the shaft by using the head (see photo 3-48).

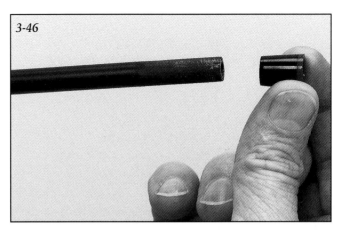

3-46

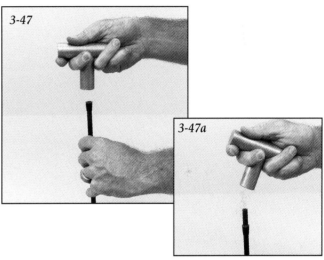

3-47

3-47a

Another ferrule installation tool is the Stock #351 Ferrule Installation Tool (see *SPECIAL NOTE:* below). To use, check the bore depth with the knurled rod (see photo 3-47b) and set the rod in place by tightening the round handle. Next, turn the tool around and with a light tapping motion, tap the ferrule onto the shaft (see photo 3-47c). This puts the ferrule at the precise point of full hosel penetration.

3-47b

SPECIAL NOTE:

When using heads with the hosel weight port you must not let the knurled rod go to the bottom of the hosel weight port. This will result in the ferrule being installed too far up the shaft. The knurled rod must go only to the bottom of the shaft bore. There is an edge or lip indicating the bottom of the hosel bore and the start of the weight port. By running the knurled rod down the inside edge of the hosel, you should be able to set the knurled rod at the proper depth on the bottom edge of the shaft bore portion of the shaft (see Diagram 3-3 for proper shafting depth).

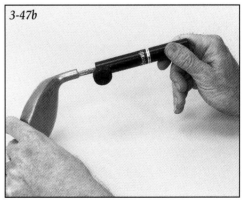

Diagram 3-3

3-47c

3-48

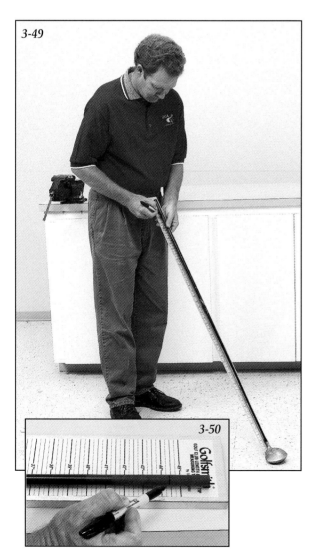

3-49

3-50

As mentioned earlier, the head can be used to install the ferrule to its full penetration. Once the ferrule has been partially installed, simply take the head and use it as the driving tool to put the ferrule in exactly the right place on the shaft. Holding the shaft firmly in one hand and the head in the other (see photo 3-48), firmly tap the butt of the shaft on a hard surface. This will drive the shaft through the ferrule and to the bottom of the bore.

NOTE: An alternative procedure is to install the ferrule at the time the head is being epoxied onto the shaft. To do this, simply dip the tip of the shaft into the epoxy mix and slide the ferrule over the tip of the shaft. You can then drive the ferrule on with the head as shown here. The head should then be removed and the proper amount of epoxy should be applied to the shaft tip and the hosel of the head. The application of the epoxy will be covered later in this section.

After driving the ferrule onto the shaft, leave the head on and measure and mark the butt end of the shaft for the final length cut. Photo 3-49 illustrates measuring the club with the 48-inch club rule (Stock #8460). Photo 3-50 illustrates measuring and marking the shaft using the True Measure Precision Golf Club Rule (Stock #4606). Be sure and mark the shaft approximately ⅛ inch to ¼ inch short of the desired final length of the club. When the grip is installed, the grip cap makes up for this amount.

When cutting any type of graphite shaft it is recommended that the shaft be taped where the cut will occur. This helps prevent any splintering of the graphite fibers during the cutting process. Photo 3 –51 illustrates taping of the butt of the shaft before cutting. In this example, use ¾-inch masking tape is used . Any width at least ¾ inch will work.

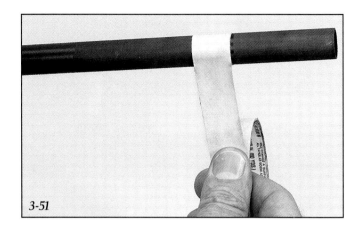

3-51

SPECIAL NOTE: *The masking tape can also be applied directly over the area to be cut. Simply put the masking tape in the general area of the cut, measure the shaft and place the cut mark on the tape. Then, simply saw or cut through the tape and the shaft.*

Photo 3-52 shows the Stock #8586 Rod Saw Blade on a standard hack saw being used to cut the graphite shaft to length. The Stock #8587 Grit – Edge Saw Blade can also be used. Place the shaft in a vise, being sure to use a shaft protecting vise clamp (Stock #8288 for shaft butts is shown) to prevent damage to the shaft in the vise. Once the shaft is securely in the vise, place the saw blade on the mark and with a normal to slow sawing motion, cut the shaft. Photo 3-52a illustrates the use of the Stock #8581 6-inch cutoff wheel on a standard bench type grinder being used to cut the butt of a graphite shaft. Simply position the shaft as shown and apply slight pressure to the blade to cut the shaft. A ⅓-hp motor is the minimum power that can be used with this cutoff wheel.

3-52

3-52a

NOTE: *Always remember to wear protective eyewear when using power equipment.*

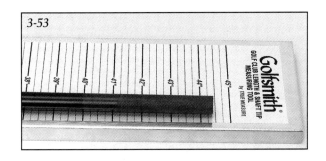

After cutting, check the length again. The photo 3-53 illustrates the shaft length after the cut is approximately ⅛ inch under the desired final length of 44.5 inches.

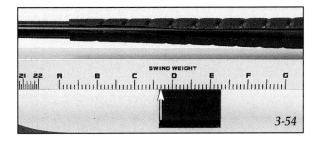

The final step before the actual assembly process begins is to check what the swingweight of the club will be. To do this, you will need an old grip that is split. The grip should be the same kind that will be used in the final assembly process, or at least one that is the same weight as the grip that will be used in the final assembly. This easily slips over the butt of the shaft. The purpose is to simulate what the final swingweight will be after assembly and to determine if any weight will need to be added during the assembly process. The head should be placed on the tip end of the shaft dry (with no epoxy), making sure the shaft goes in the head to the bottom of the bore. Since the ferrule is pre-set, you can tell when the head is on properly. Now, check the swingweight reading (see photo 3-54). In this example, notice that the swingweight is approximately C8.

SPECIAL NOTE: Measuring the swingweight of a golf club prior to and after assembly is not required in the assembly process. For a definition of swingweight and its function, refer to the Appendix and the Glossary of clubmaking terms. Golfsmith sells several models of swingweight scales. The one pictured is the Model 15006. There is also the model 14009. See the Golfsmith Components Catalog for pricing.

Before you can epoxy the shaft into the head, you must clean out the hosel. This is necessary to clean out any dirt, oil, etc. that may have been left in the hosel during the manufacturing process. The first recommended step is to use a Flex Hone Tool (Stock #8625). As illustrated in photo 3-55, the silicon carbide bristles on the Flex Hone Tool are pushed into the hosel with a twisting motion. This will remove or loosen unwanted material in the hosel. It also roughs up the inside of the hosel, which aids in the adhesion process. The next step is to take cotton swabs (see photo 3-55a), dip them into some acetone and swab out the hosel. This will clean out the entire remaining residue. Once you have swabbed out the hosel with acetone, set it aside to dry for a few minutes.

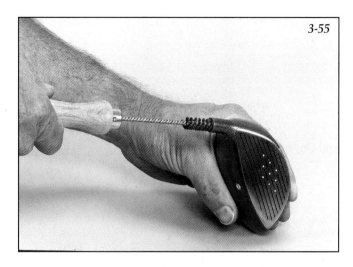

3-55

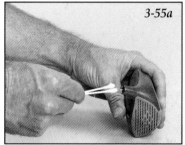

3-55a

SPECIAL NOTE:

All of the heads in the Golfsmith catalog have been designed with a special "coning" or beveling on the inside top of the hosel. This is necessary to prevent premature graphite shaft failure caused by a sharp edge against a graphite shaft at the top of the hosel. If you are using a head that is not coned, and are shafting with a graphite shaft, you will have to cone or bevel the top of the hosel. This requires the use of a 20-degree Countersink (Stock #794) bit in a hand drill (see figure 1). After the coning operation is done, Sandstone Coning Bit (Stock #8785) can be used to smooth out the burrs caused by the coning operation. This is only necessary on heads that have not been, or have insufficient coning when they are going to be shafted with a graphite shaft (see figure 2).

figure 1

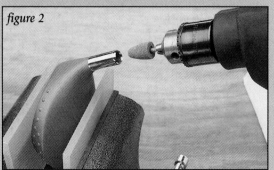

figure 2

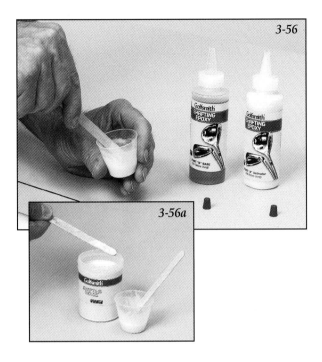

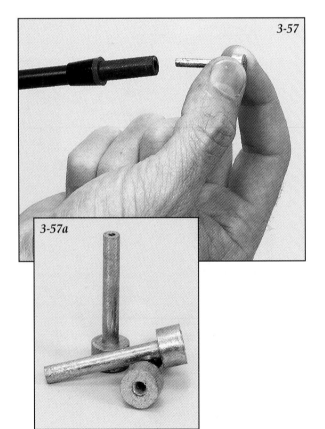

SPECIAL NOTE: This is a very important step. Many epoxy bond failures are due to contaminants in the epoxy that come from the hosel.

It's time to epoxy the head onto the shaft. There are two types of epoxy that can be used equally well with graphite shafts—the Golfsmith Shafting Epoxy (Stock #9095 for 10 oz. quantity) or the Golfsmith Standard Shafting Epoxy (Stock #9095 for half-pint size). It is best to use mixing cups similar to the one pictured. The Graphite Shafting Epoxy, Stock #995, mixes 2 parts activator (Part A) to 3 parts base (Part B). If using this epoxy, simply pour out the proper amounts of Part A and Part B in separate cups, then mix together. If using the Stock #9095 Standard Golfsmith Epoxy, simply pour out equal amounts of Part A and Part B into separate cups (mixes to a 1 to 1 ratio), then mix together. It is very important to mix thoroughly. Mix for at least one minute. Mix until the epoxy is a consistent color throughout (see photo 3-56). Photo inset 3-56a shows a product called epoxy beads. They are tiny glass beads that can be added to epoxy for to insure adequate epoxy cushion between the shaft and hosel wall. These beads can eliminate the possibility of shafting a club off-center. If the shaft is a loose fit in the hosel, we recommend using these beads (Stock #9082). If the shaft is a good fit and does not lean when put into the hosel, the beads are not necessary.

If weight needs to added for swingweighting purposes, there are a couple of methods to consider. Photo 3-57 shows a graphite shaft tip weight. They come in a variety of weights (two gram to five gram, see photo inset 3-57a) and are available in the Golfsmith Components Catalog. These weights are installed at the time of assembly and simply slip into the tip of the shaft.

In some cases, depending on the type of graphite shaft, the shaft tip weights may not fit into the tip of the shaft. In those cases, you can use a small drill bit (⅛ inch) and ream out the tip of the shaft. You must be very careful not to damage the fibers of the shaft. In photo 3-58, the shaft has been secured into a vise using a Protective Shaft Clamp (Stock #8288). Using a standard hand drill and a ⅛-inch drill bit, slowly ream out the tip of the shaft. Only go into the shaft the amount necessary to allow the tip weight proper penetration.

3-58

After reaming the tip of the shaft, test fit the tip weight (see photo 3-59).

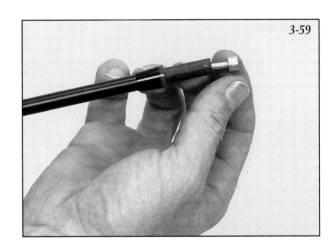

3-59

As photo 3-59 shows, these shaft tip weights have a head on them that will add approximately ¼ inch to the length of the club. Because of this, it will be necessary to trim that amount from the tip of the shaft (see photo 3-60). Follow the same procedures as you did when trimming the tip, taping the area to be cut and using either the hacksaw with the rod saw blade in the photo, or with a cut off wheel. It is also possible to simply grind or file the tip. A 30-inch or 42-inch belt sander with a medium grit belt will also do the trick. Whichever method you use, the shaft tip should be taped with masking tape to prevent damage to the graphite fibers.

3-60

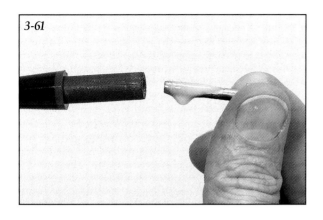

3-61

Once the shaft is ready for assembly, dip the tip weight into the epoxy mix and insert into the tip of the shaft (see photo 3-61). This is done just before the head is to be installed.

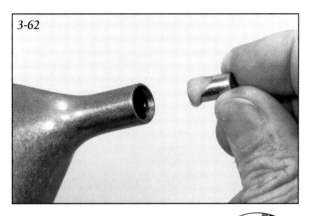

3-62

Many of the heads in the Golfsmith Components Catalog are designed with a hosel weight port, which allows a special lead or tungsten weight plug to be installed into the bottom of the hosel. As with the shaft tip weights, this allows for increasing the swingweight at the time of assembly. To install, simply coat the weight in epoxy and drop in the hosel (see photo 3-62). Be sure the weight falls all the way to the bottom of the weight port (see Diagram 3-4).

Diagram 3-4
Proper Position of Hosel Bore
Weight in Head.

SPECIAL NOTE: When the head does have the hosel weight port feature, this is the preferred method.

It's time to install the shaft. Using a mixing stick, put a small bead of epoxy on the inside of the hosel (see photo 3-63). Do not fill the hosel. A small amount is all that is necessary.

3-63

Next, take the mixing stick and coat the outside of the tip of the shaft with epoxy (see photo 3-64). Be sure to get a good coverage over the tip of the shaft.

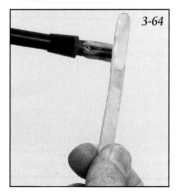

3-64

One option, instead of using the mixing stick, is to simply dip the shaft tip into the epoxy mix as shown in photo 3-65. Again, be sure you get good coverage on the outside of the shaft tip.

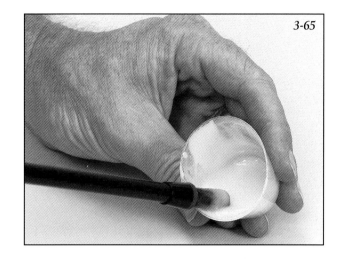

Once the shaft tip is thoroughly coated, you can use it to spread the epoxy on the inside of the hosel (see photo 3-66).

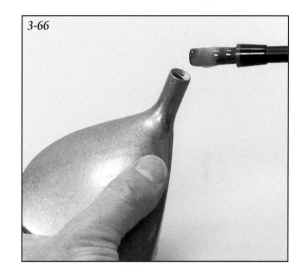

Install the shaft by inserting it into the hosel, slowly rotating or twisting the shaft as it goes into the hosel. Once you have the shaft all the in the hosel, pull the shaft about half way out, still rotating it, and re-insert the shaft all the way (see photo 3-67). This insures that epoxy is covering every area inside the hosel and on the shaft tip.

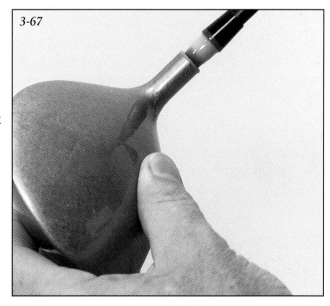

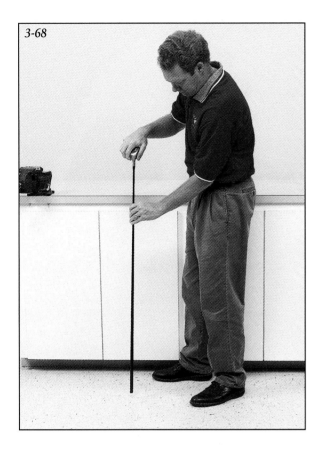

3-68

Turn the club upside down and gently tap the butt of the shaft on a hard surface (see photo 3-68). Do not tap the butt on vinyl, wood or tile floors. A concrete floor, metal block or scrap wood block used as the hard surface is recommended. This helps insure the shaft is inserted all the way to the bottom of the hosel.

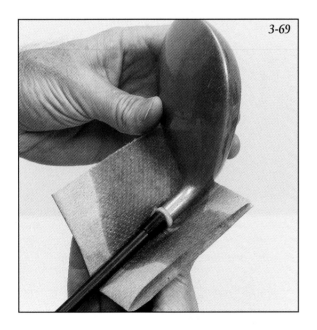

3-69

Using a paper towel dampened with solvent, wipe the excess epoxy off of the hosel and ferrule area (see photo 3-69). It is much easier to wipe this area clean when the epoxy is still wet, so be meticulous. Get it as clean as possible.

Set the club upright, as shown in photo 3-70, for curing. The Golfsmith Graphite shafting epoxy, Stock #995 and the Golfsmith Standard shafting epoxy, Stock #9095, are 24-hour cure epoxies. Although the epoxies actual gel time may be shorter, it is not recommended that the club be used for at least 24 hours. The epoxy mix that is not used leave out in the mixing cup. It will be your reference to see if the epoxy has cured. The Golfsmith 24-hour epoxy will be very hard when it cures. If the epoxy is cured correctly, it should appear hard and if pressed firmly with a mixing stick, should leave little, if any indentation.

SPECIAL NOTE: Outside temperatures can effect the curing time. The warmer it is, the faster and harder the epoxy cures. It is still recommended no club be used for a minimum of 24 hours after assembly.

After the proper cure time has past, check the epoxy mix left in the cup (see photo 3-71).

Next, check the head for tightness (see photo 3-72).

If the club you have assembled has a ferrule, the ferrule portion of the club may need finishing or cleaning up after the assembly is complete. Most ferrules will be slightly larger than the outside diameter of the hosel. To get a clean, professional look, it is recommended that the ferrule be "turned down" or smoothed so it is the same diameter of the hosel. If a belt sander is not available, the ferrule can be turned down by hand. Use masking tape to cover the shaft and hosel. Sand the ferrule down using a file and a fine grit sand paper. This procedure can also be done using a linen-polishing belt on a 30-inch or 42-inch belt sander. (see photo 3-73) Pictured is a close-up of Stock #8209 ferrule turning support arm and the Stock #446 1 X 42 inch belt sander with motor). Care must be taken not to

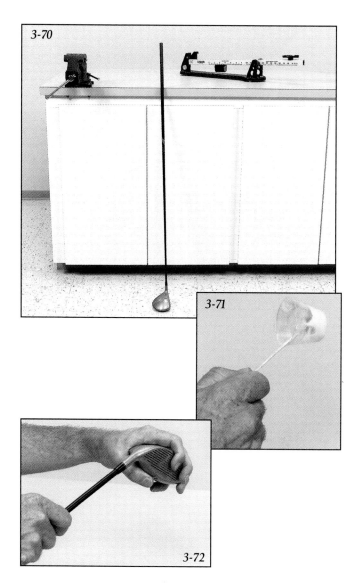

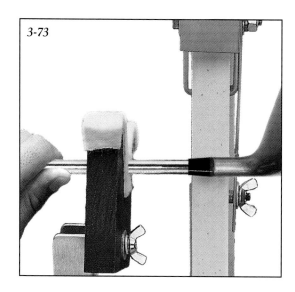

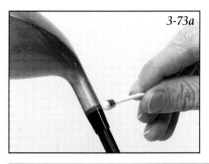

3-73a

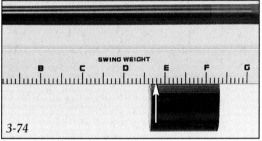

SWING WEIGHT

B C D E F G

3-74

See SPECIAL NOTES on page 59
before proceeding.

3-75

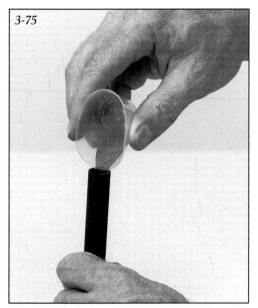

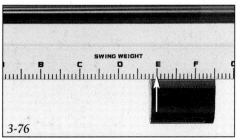

SWING WEIGHT

B C D E F C

3-76

damage the finish of the head or the ferrule itself. Now use the acetone. If the ferrule is almost flush with the hosel, you can skip this procedure, simply go to applying acetone to the ferrule with a cotton swab or a paper towel. This will give the ferrule a nice shine (see photo 3-73a).

One method of fine tuning the swingweight of the club after the head is assembled is to add weight down the shaft using lead or tungsten powder (see page 38 about shafts with SensiCore). Before you actually add the lead, you must check the swingweight of the club without the grip on (see photo 3-74). swingweight readings without a grip on the club will be approximately 10 swingweights points higher than the actual final swingweight will be. For example, the photo shows the swingweight of this club to be D8 without the grip. If we did nothing but put a standard rubber grip on without adding any weight, the final swingweight of this club would be around C8.

To use the lead or tungsten powder, measure out the amount of lead powder (Stock #9466) you want to add and pour it down the shaft. Two grams equals approximately one swingweight point. Once you have poured the lead powder into the butt end of the shaft (see photo 3-75), tap the club gently against a hard surface to insure the powder is all the way to the bottom of the shaft. It is recommended that no more than eight to 10 grams be added down the shaft using this method. More than that amount could effect the playability of the club.

Recheck the swingweight without a grip.

SPECIAL NOTE: in the example (photo 3-76) the swingweight is now E0. Place the split grip on the club and check the swingweight. In this example, the reading is now D0 (see photo 3-76a on page 59).

Once the desired amount of weight is added, a cork must be epoxied down the shaft to prevent the lead powder from coming out of the shaft. Graphite wood shafts require Stock #882C in the Golfsmith Component Catalog. Apply regular shafting epoxy to the cork and drop it into the butt end of the shaft (see photo 3-77). Be sure to drop the tapered end of the cork into the shaft first.

Using a Ram Rod for graphite shafts (Stock #8645), firmly push the cork down to the tip end of the shaft. Remove the rod from the shaft (see photo 3-78).

There will usually be some lead powder that remains loose in the shaft after the cork is installed. You want to remove this from the shaft. Simply turn the shaft butt down and tap firmly on a hard surface. The powder residue should all come out the butt of the shaft (see photo 3-79).

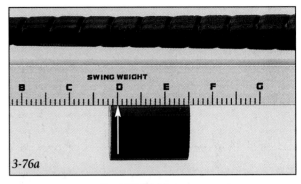

3-76a

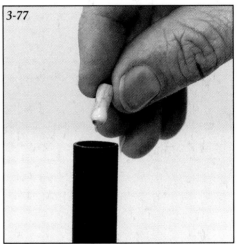

3-77

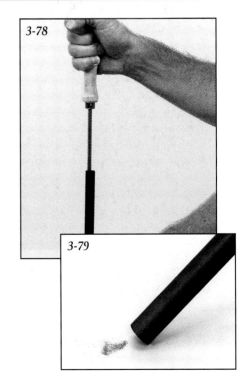

3-78

3-79

SPECIAL NOTE:

It is not recommended that this be done in addition to shaft tip weights or hosel weight port weights. This should be done as an alternative method. Also you should place a Ram Rod down the graphite shaft to see how far down additional lead weight and a cork will go.

The inside diameters of some graphite shafts may be too small, not allowing the weight or the cork to be installed in the proper position. Also, if the club is being made to a final club length longer than 46 inches, the Ram Rod may not go to the bottom of the shaft, which would prevent using this method.

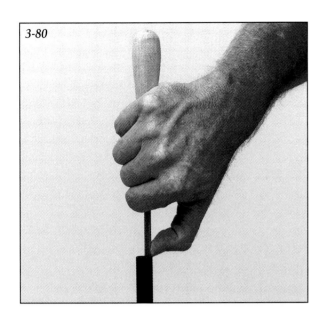

3-80

It is important to make sure that the cork is in the proper place inside the shaft. To check the corks position, put the Ram Rod back into the shaft as far down as it will go. Mark the shaft with a marker or your thumb (see photo 3-80) and remove the rod.

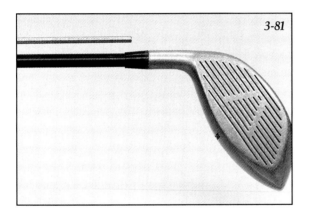

3-81

Place the Ram Rod along side the outside of the club and check the depth. Photo 3-81 shows a close up of the rod tip and the approximate depth the cork is in the shaft. It is not recommended that the cork be above the hosel/ferrule line. Any epoxy or epoxied piece of material inside the shaft that is above the hosel/ferrule line could cause the shaft to prematurely fail.

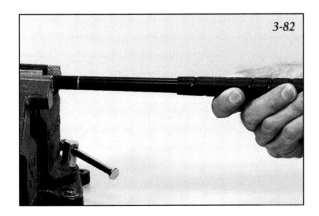

3-82

Install the grip (see photo 3-82). For complete gripping instructions, see Chapter 2.

Re-check length of the club after the grip is installed. In this example, the final length is 44½ inches (see photo 3-83).

Re-check swingweight. In this example, the final swingweight is D0 (see photo 3-84).

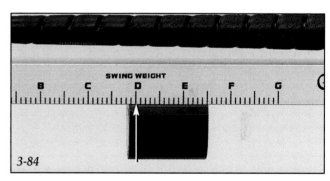

List of Supplies Needed for Metal Wood Assembly

- ❏ Golf club components – head, shaft, grip, ferrule *(if necessary)*
- ❏ ¾-inch or 2-inch two sided grip tape
- ❏ Non – flammable grip solvent
- ❏ Shafting epoxy
- ❏ Mixing Cups and Sticks
- ❏ Shaft cutting tools: Stock #858 Shaft Cutter or Stock #8581 Cutoff Wheel for steel shafts, Stock #'s 8587, 8586 Saw Blades or Stock #8581 Cutoff Wheel for graphite shafts
- ❏ Pro Metal Vise Clamps: Stock #8288 for shaft butts, Stock #8288 for shaft tips and general use
- ❏ 48-Inch Combination Ruler – Stock #8460 or True Measure Precision Golf Club Rule – Stock #4606
- ❏ Coarse grit sandpaper for prepping steel shafts, surface conditioning belt for graphite shafts
- ❏ Knife for prepping Graphite shafts
- ❏ Hosel Cleaning Brush Set for cleaning hosels, Stock #8625for irons, Stock #8625 for woods
- ❏ Cotton swabs - Acetone (Buy Locally)
- ❏ Bench Vise

List of Optional Supplies for Metal Wood Assembly

- ❏ 30-inch or 42-inch Belt Sander for use in shaft prepping of steel and Graphite shafts
  -optional
- ❏ Mr. T Ferrule Installer, Stock #8296 or Ferrule Installation Tool, Stock #351 *-optional*
- ❏ Swingweight Scale *-optional*
- ❏ Shaft tip weights for steel and graphite shafts, hosel weight port weights*-optional*
- ❏ Lead Powder (Stock #9466 Tungsten) and Corks (Stock #882 A, C) *-optional*
- ❏ Epoxy Beads, Stock #9082 *-optional*
- ❏ Split grip for swingweighting purposes *-optional*

Chapter 4

Assembly for Irons and Wedges

The processes involved in assembling irons and wedges are the same. The difference comes in which irons and which wedges are right for you. In the last 10 years or so there has been a lot of emphasis placed on the importance of set make-up. Many players are discovering that they do not need long irons (1-, 2- or 3-iron) in their bag because they simply cannot hit them well. These are being replaced, in some cases, by higher-lofted woods. These higher-lofted woods are often times easier to hit for the players than the long irons. On the other end of the set, in the short irons, the strong lofts on most sets manufactured today have created distance gaps. For instance, 25 years ago a standard pitching wedge loft was around 50 to 52 degrees. Today, the average pitching wedge loft is closer to 47 to 48 degrees. With the lofts of sand wedges remaining in the 55 to 56 degree range, as they have traditionally been, a distance gap is created between the pitching wedge and the sand wedge. Because of this, additional "gap" wedges have become popular to help round out a player's short game arsenal. In addition, high lob wedges have become popular to help players of all levels hit the difficult high, soft pitch shots that are needed from time to time around the greens. With this recognition by many players that the traditional set make up does not do the most for their game, new combinations of irons and wedges are becoming more the norm. It is not uncommon, and in fact is recommended in many cases, to see iron sets starting with the 4- or 5-iron and including three and sometimes four wedges. The point of all this is to encourage you to be creative in your iron selection and set make-up so that you have the best clubs in your bag to help you lower your score. It makes no sense to have clubs in you bag you either do not like to hit or can not hit well.

Obviously, before you can begin to assemble an iron or a wedge, you have to choose what type you want. Golfsmith offers a wide range of styles in both irons and wedges. In irons, there is the traditional look of the Golfsmith Forged Blade (played by Scott Verplank on the PGA Tour) and the Tour Cavity (played by Bruce Lietzke on the PGA Tour). If you prefer the game improvement variety, the XPC3, 15-5 stainless midsize models offer, cavity back features that are solid and forgiving on off-center hits. There are many other midsize cavity-back options, along with some of the most advanced bi-metal and tri-metal designs in golf. (**NOTE:** *By combining different materials into one design, it is possible to achieve a weight distribution that is simply not possible with a one-material design*). All of the clubheads in the Golfsmith Component Catalog are tested for performance and durability. A wide variety of cosmetic options are included in these designs. When choosing what head you want to build, look at not only the features of the design and the benefits that it may offer, also pay attention to the overall look of the club. If you do not like the way the head looks, chances are you will not hit it as good as one that appeals to you aesthetically.

Since wedge head assembly is included here, we might as well include some tips in selecting the right wedges for your game. As with the iron models, Golfsmith carries a wide variety of wedge options. The two main features of the wedges to consider are the loft of the club and the sole angle, or bounce, of the clubhead. The loft determines the backspin and trajectory of the shot, along with the distance it will travel. Choose a loft that allows you to hit shots the correct distance with the correct trajectory without having to manipulate the face angle, or the amount of loft on the club (i.e.: open or close the blade). Ideally, you want a progression of distance built into your wedges, where the pitching wedge give you one distance and trajectory, the sand wedge gives you another distance and trajectory, and if needed, a lob wedge gives you another distance and trajectory. As mentioned before, if yardage gaps occur, for instance between your pitching wedge and sand wedge, a gap wedge may be in order. The main thing is to try and maintain a progression of lofts of approximately four to five and no more than seven degrees of loft in the wedges to cover all the distance requirements. The bounce or sole angle of the club can be designed on the wedges to help prevent fat or thin shots from occurring in a variety of turf conditions. The results, however, are highly dependent on the ability of the player. Simply put, the wider the sole and the more the bounce, the softer the turf conditions need to be for the optimum result. The narrower the sole and the less the bounce, the firmer or tighter the turf conditions need to be for optimum results. When choosing the wedge make-up for your set, pay attention to the loft and the bounce specifications listed in the catalog, and make your choice based on these guidelines.

The first part of this chapter will cover assembling a steel shaft into an iron head. If you have put together metal woods with steel shafts or putters with steel shafts before, the procedures are very similar. The second part of the chapter involves shafting an iron head (actually a sand wedge head) with a graphite shaft. Understand, the procedures for putting steel or graphite shaft in an iron head, whether it be a 5-iron or a sand wedge, are the same. Be sure and read through all of the procedures for the job before you start. Even if you have done this before, we recommend you follow the steps completely, taking no short cuts. These are time proven methods. If you have any questions, contact Golfsmith customer service at 800-925-7709 or visit any of our Retail locations for assistance.

Be sure and read through all of the procedures for the job before you start.

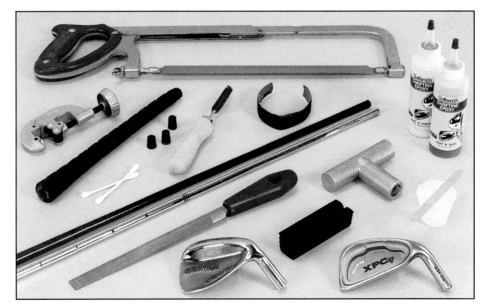

Supplies for Assembling Irons and Wedges

STEEL SHAFTS

The first step to assembling an iron head with a steel shaft is to trim the shaft tip according to the manufacturers recommended trimming instructions. Before cutting the tip of the shaft, mark the amount that must be trimmed from the tip. Photo 4-1 shows marking this particular shaft at the two inch mark.

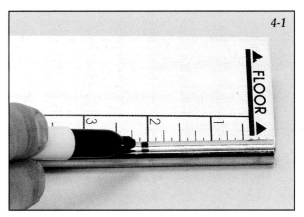

There are several ways to cut a steel shaft. Photo 4-2 shows the use of the Super Shaft Cutter (Stock #858). To use this cutter, simply loosen the knob and place it over the shaft tip, aligning the blade directly on the line marking the spot of the cut. Gently tighten the cutting tool by turning the knob. Once the blade is securely tight on the shaft, begin rotating the blade around the shaft. If the blade slides off of the mark, re-position and tighten. After rotating the cutting tool around the shaft a few times, tighten the knob tighter. Continue to rotate the blade, tightening after several rotations. When the cut is complete, the shaft tip should break off clean at the intended cut line. There may be small burrs created from the cut. If so, you can use a medium or fine hand cutting file or sand paper to remove or debur these edges. An alternative method (photo 4-2a) is to use a cutoff wheel (Stock #8581), which attaches to a bench grinder or electric motor (minimum ⅓ hp motor). This wheel is designed to cut steel or graphite shafts quickly and efficiently. **If this method is used, be sure to wear protective eyewear.**

After cutting the shaft, test fit the shaft into the hosel. To insure that the shaft is going all the way in to the bottom of the bore, it is important to know what the total bore depth is of the head. You can determine this by taking a pencil or something similar and putting it into the hosel. Mark the depth then pull the pencil out, lay it next to the shaft and mark the shaft. This will tell you the depth the shaft must go into the head **. Photo 4-3 shows the shaft inserted into the head. Notice the ¾-inch masking

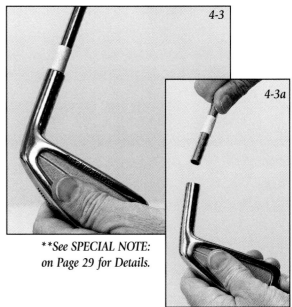

***See SPECIAL NOTE:** on Page 29 for Details.*

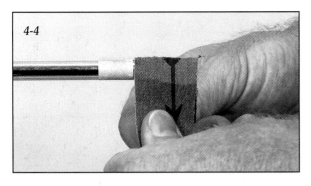

4-4

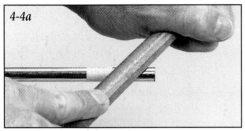

4-4a

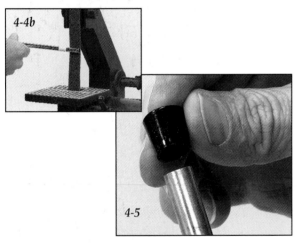

4-4b

4-5

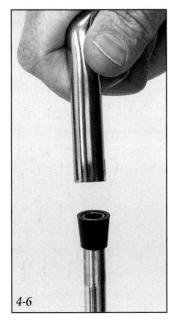

4-6

tape that has been applied on the shaft at the top of the hosel. This tape not only marks the shaft for the proper bore depth, but it also protects the shaft during the abrading process. Once you have the shaft in the head and the shaft is marked (or taped), remove the shaft from the head (photo 4-3a). **NOTE:** *In some cases the shaft may not slide easily into the head. Do not force the shaft into the head. If the shaft will not slide into the shaft, go ahead and abrade the tip of the shaft (see photo 4-4, 4-4a, 4-4b for different methods of preparing the shaft). Procedures for all three methods will follow).* Many times removing the chrome from the tip is all it takes to make the shaft fit.

Its time to abrade or "rough up" the tip of the shaft. Take coarse grit sandpaper and cut it into approximately a one inch wide x five or six inch long strip. Place the shaft in a vise (use Protective Shaft Clamp Stock- #8249 or Rubber Vise Clamp Stock- #913) and secure it. If the head is a style that requires a ferrule, you can abrade slightly above the hosel line. As shown in photo 4-4, place the strip over the tip of the shaft and work the sandpaper back and forth. You will need to rotate the shaft so that all sides of the tip are abraded. Once the shaft tip is completely abraded, clean the tip with a damp cloth. An alternative method is to use a fine cut file as shown in photo 4-4a. You can also use a 30-inch or 42-inch belt sander with a medium or coarse grit belt as shown in photo 4-4b. Be sure to wear protective eyewear when using any type of power equipment. The belt sanders and the belts are available through Golfsmith.

If the head requires a ferrule, it can be installed onto the shaft prior to epoxying the head in place or at the time the head is installed. To install the ferrule without epoxy, first place the ferrule over the tip of the shaft (see photo 4-5).

Next, take the head, as shown in photo 4-6, and push the ferrule down into position. This puts the ferrule into the exact correct position on the shaft. One handy tool you can use to install the ferrule is the Mr. T Ferrule installer (Stock #8690). To use, simply place the ferrule on the tip of the shaft as in photo 4-6a. Place the tool over the ferrule and press firmly down. The ferrule is then set approximately one inch onto the shaft (see photo 4-6b). Once this is done, then you can use the hosel of the clubhead to drive the ferrule down the shaft tip to the exact full penetration depth.

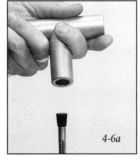

4-6a

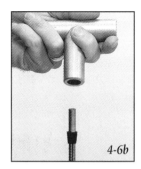

4-6b

Another ferrule installation tool you can use is the Stock #351 Ferrule Installation Tool. To use, check the bore depth with the knurled rod (see photo 4-7) and then set the rod in place by tightening the round knob. See *SPECIAL NOTE* on page 29 for additional instructions. Next, turn the tool around and with a light tapping motion tap the ferrule onto the shaft (see photo 4-7a). This puts the ferrule at the precise point of full hosel penetration. See page 47 for instructions.

4-7

4-7a

Once the ferrule is installed, put the head on the shaft without any epoxy, and mark the shaft for cutting to final length (see photo 4-8). If the head will not stay on the head, you can put a small piece of masking tape on the tip of the shaft to help hold the head in place while measuring. Be sure the head is all the way on the shaft. If it is not, the final length cut will be incorrect.

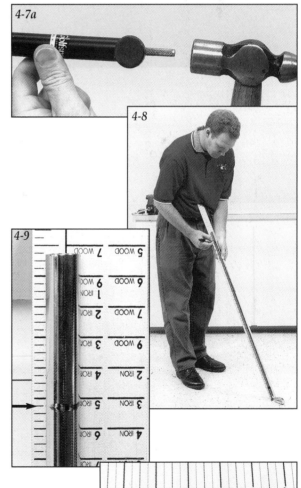

4-8

4-9

Photo 4-9 shows a close-up of the cut mark on the shaft. In this case, the shaft is being cut at a standard 5-iron length (38-inch). Notice how the mark is approximately ⅛ of an inch below the desired final club length mark for a 5-iron. This allows for the added length added to the club by the grip. Usually the a standard slip on rubber or composition grip will add ⅛ inch to ¼ inch to the club length. Photo 4-9a shows the same operation using the Stock #4606 True Measure Club Rule.

After the shaft is marked place the shaft securely in a vise. Be sure to use a rubber vise clamp to protect the shaft.

4-9a

4-10

4-10a

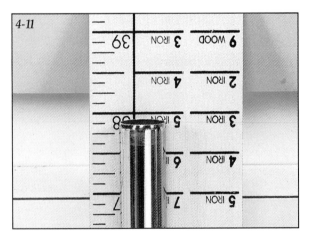

4-11

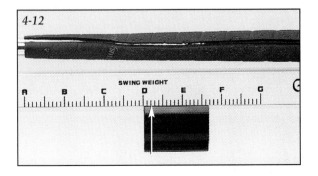

4-12

Place the Super Shaft Cutter (Stock #858) around the butt of the shaft as shown in photo 4-10. Place the blade right on the designated cut mark. Gently tighten the cutting tool by turning the knob. Once the blade is tight on the shaft, begin rotating the blade around the shaft. If the blade slides off the mark, re-position and tighten. After rotating the cutting tool around the shaft a few times, tighten the knob again. Continue to rotate the blade, tightening after several rotations. When the cut is complete, the shaft tip should break off clean at the intended cut line. There may be small burrs created from the cut. If so, you can use a medium or fine hand cutting file or sand paper to remove or debur these edges. An alternative method to cut the shaft (photo 4-10a) is to use a cutoff wheel (Stock #8581), which attaches to a bench grinder or electric motor (minimum ⅓ hp motor). This wheel is designed to cut steel or graphite shafts quickly and efficiently. If this method is used, be sure to wear protective eyewear. Photo 4-11 is a close up view of the butt of the shaft after the cut.

The final step before the actual assembly process begins is to check to see what the swingweight of the club will be. To do this, you will need an old grip that is split. The grip should be the same kind that will be used in the final assembly process, or at least one that is the same weight as the grip that will be used in the final assembly. This easily slips over the butt of the shaft. The purpose is to simulate what the final swingweight will be after assembly and to determine if any weight will need to be added during the assembly process. The head should be placed on the tip end of the shaft dry (with no epoxy), making sure the shaft goes in the head to the bottom of the bore. Since the ferrule is pre-set, you can tell when the head is on properly. Now, check the swingweight reading (see photo 4-12). In this example note the swingweight is approximately D2. **NOTE:** *Measuring the swingweight of a golf club prior to and after assembly is not required in the assembly process.* For a definition of swingweight and its function, refer to the Appendix and the Glossary of clubmaking terms. Golfsmith sells several models of swingweight scales. The one pictured is the Model 15006. There is also the model 14009. See the Golfsmith Components Catalog for pricing. See diagram 4-1 on page 84 for proper position of weight.

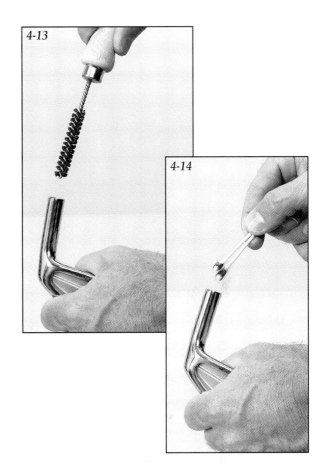

4-13

4-14

Before you can epoxy the shaft into the head, you must clean out the hosel. This is necessary to clean out any dirt, oil, etc. that may have been left in the hosel during the manufacturing process. The first recommended step is to use a Flex Hone Tool (Stock #750). As illustrated in photo 4-13, the silicon carbide bristles on the Flex Hone Tool are pushed into the hosel with a twisting motion. This will remove or loosen unwanted material in the hosel. It also roughs up the inside of the hosel, which aids in the adhesion process.

The next step is to take cotton swabs (see photo 4-14), dip them into acetone and swab out the hosel. This will clean out the remaining residue. Once you have swabbed out the hosel with acetone, set it aside for a few minutes to dry. Note: This is a very important step. Many epoxy bond failures are due to contaminants in the epoxy that come from the hosel.

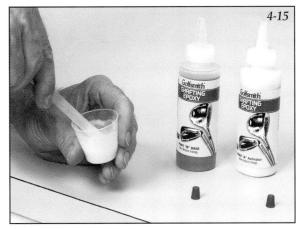

4-15

It's time to epoxy the head onto the shaft. We recommend using the Golfsmith Shafting Epoxy (Stock #9095 for half-pint quantity). Parts A and B mix at a 1 : 1 ratio. It is best to use mixing cups similar to the one pictured. Simply pour out equal amounts of Part A and Part B in separate cups, then mix together. It is very important to mix thoroughly. Mix for at least one minute. Mix until the epoxy until it is a consistent color throughout (see photo 4-15). Photo inset 4-15a shows a product called epoxy beads. They are tiny glass beads that can be added to epoxy to insure adequate epoxy cushion between the shaft and hosel wall. These beads can eliminate the possibility of shafting a club off-center. If the shaft is a loose fit in the hosel, we recommend using these beads (Stock #9082). If the shaft is a good fit and does not

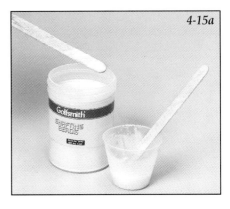

4-15a

lean when put into the hosel, the beads are not necessary.

If weight needs to be added for swingweighting purposes, there are a couple of methods of doing this. Photo 4-16 shows a shaft tip weight being installed in the tip of the shaft. These type weights are available in various weights in the Golfsmith Components Catalog. If using these type of weights, simply coat the inside of the shaft tip with a small amount of epoxy, dip the weight in the epoxy and insert the weight into the tip of the shaft.

Many of the heads in the Golfsmith catalog are designed with the hosel weight port, which allows a special lead or tungsten weight plug to be installed into the bottom of the hosel. As with the shaft tip weights, this allows for increasing the swingweight at the time of assembly. To install , simply coat the weight in epoxy and drop in the hosel (see photo 4-17). Be sure the weight falls all the way to the bottom of the weight port (see diagram 3-2 on page 35 for proper positioning of the weight.

It's time to install the shaft. Using a mixing stick, put a small bead of epoxy on the inside of the hosel (see photo 4-18). Do not fill the hosel. A small amount is all that is necessary.

Next, take the mixing stick and coat the outside of the tip of the shaft with epoxy (see photo 4-19). Be sure to get a good coverage over the tip of the shaft.

One option, instead of using the mixing stick, is to simply dip the shaft tip into the epoxy mix as shown in photo 4-20. Again, be sure you get good coverage on the outside of the shaft tip.

Once the shaft is thoroughly coated, you can use it to spread the epoxy on the inside of the hosel (see photo 4-21).

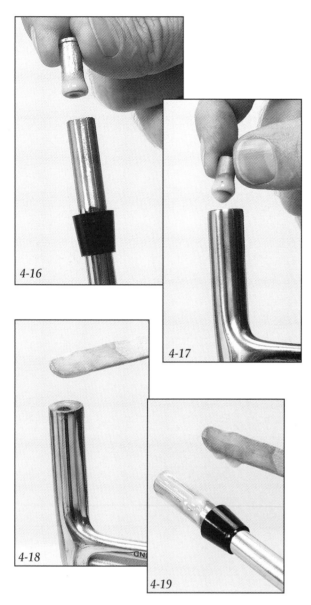

4-16

4-17

4-18

4-19

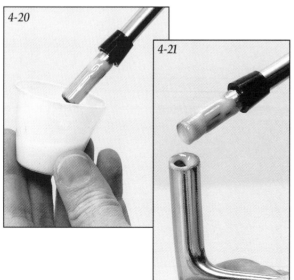

4-20

4-21

Install the shaft by inserting it into the hosel, slowly rotating or twisting the shaft as it goes into the hosel (see photo 4-22). Once you have the shaft all the way in the hosel, pull the shaft about half way out, still rotating it, and re-insert the shaft all the way. This insures that epoxy is covering every area inside the hosel and on the shaft tip.

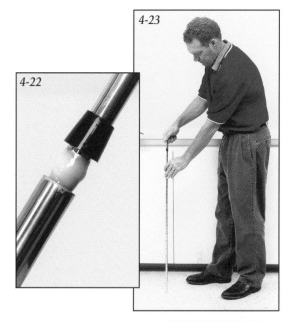

Turn the club upside down and gently tap the butt of the shaft on a hard surface (see photo 4-23). Do not tap the butt on vinyl, wood or tile floors. A concrete floor, metal block or scrap wood block used as the hard surface is recommended. This helps insure the shaft is inserted all the way to the bottom of the hosel.

Using a paper towel dampened with solvent, wipe the excess epoxy off of the hosel and ferrule area (see photo 4-24). It is much easier to wipe this area clean when the epoxy is still wet, so be meticulous. Get it as clean as possible. Set the club upright, as shown in photo 4-24a, for curing. The Golfsmith Epoxy, Stock #9095, is a 24-hour cure epoxy. Although actual epoxy gel time may be shorter, it is not recommended that the club be used for at least 24 hours. The epoxy mix that is not used should be left out in the mixing cup. It will be your reference to see if the epoxy has cured.

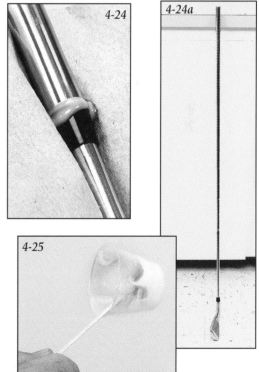

After the appropriate time for curing has past (approximately 24-hours), check the mixing cup to see if the mix used for the club has cured (see photo 4-25). If the epoxy in the cup appears soft and not cured, do not hit the club. Cure rates can vary depending on the outside temperature. At room temperature, 24 hours should be sufficient. The Golfsmith 24 hour epoxy will be very hard when it cures. If the epoxy is cured correctly, it should appear hard and if pressed firmly with a mixing stick, should leave little, if any indentation. Check the head for tightness (see photo 4-26).

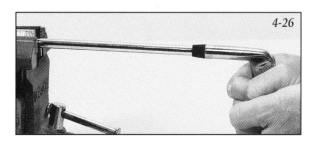

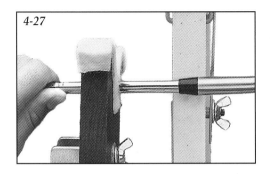
4-27

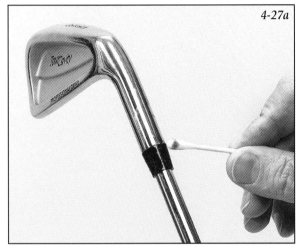
4-27a

If the club you have assembled has a ferrule, the ferrule portion of the club may need finishing or cleaning up after the assembly is complete. Most ferrules will be slightly larger than outside diameter of the hosel. To get a clean, professional look, it is recommended that the ferrule be " turned down" or smoothed so it is the same diameter of the hosel. This can be done using a linen-polishing belt on a 30-inch or 42-inch belt sander (see photo 4-27). Special care must be taken not to damage the ferrule by over sanding. If you use a 30-inch or 42-inch belt sander, we recommend you practice on a few old clubs before you start. If a belt sander is not available, the ferrule can be turned down by hand. Use masking tape to cover the shaft and hosel. Sand the ferrule down using a file and a fine grit sand paper. Photo 4-27 shows the Stock #8209 ferrule turning support arm with the 42-inch belt sander with motor. If the ferrule is almost flush with the hosel, you can skip this procedure and simply go to applying acetone to the ferrule with a cotton swabs or a paper towel (see photo 4-27a). This will smooth out the ferrule and give the ferrule a glossy shine. If you do sand the ferrule, follow with the acetone treatment.

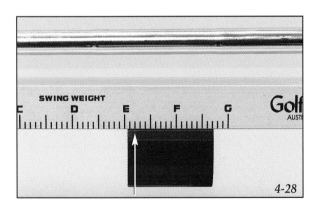
SWING WEIGHT
4-28

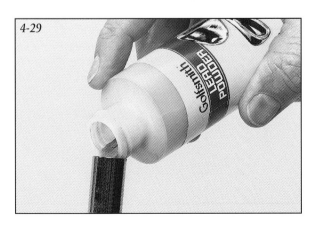
4-29

One method of fine tuning the swingweight of the club after the head is assembled is to add weight down the shaft using lead powder. *NOTE: SensiCore™ is a frequency dampening core in some steel and graphite shafts that reduces uncomfortable vibration from shots hit off the sweet spot. Because this core is inserted into the inside of the shaft, clubs made with these shafts cannot have the swingweight adjusted by inserting lead powder or other weight through the butt end of the shaft. The SensiCore insert will not allow the passage of these materials nor will it allow a Ram Rod or Long Hot Rod through the shaft.* Before you actually add the lead, you must check the swingweight of the club without the grip on (see photo 4-28). swingweight readings without a grip on the club will be approximately 10 swingweight points higher than the actual final swingweight will be. For example, the photo shows the swingweight of this club to be E2 without the grip. If we did nothing but put a standard rubber grip on without adding any weight, the final swingweight of this club would be around D2.

To increase the swingweight using lead powder (Stock #942), simply pour the lead powder into the butt end of the shaft (see photo 4-29). It will flow down to the tip end, or head end of the club. You can pre-measure in a mixing cup and weigh on a scale to predetermine how much weight you are adding. Two grams is equivalent to one swingweight point. It is not recommended that more than eight to ten grams of weight be added using this method. More than this amount could effect the playability of the club. Once you have poured the powder into the hosel, gently tap the club against a hard surface with the head end on the ground to ensure the powder goes all the way to the tip of the shaft.

After adding the powder, set the club back on the swingweight scale to check the weight (see photo 4-30). In this example, two swingweight points were added (four grams). The scale now reads E4, which, when the grip is installed, will give a final swingweight reading of approximately D4.

Once the desired amount of weight is added, a cork must be epoxied down the shaft to prevent the lead powder from coming out. There are different types for corks for different types of shafts. Steel irons shafts require Stock #882B in the Golfsmith Components Catalog. As shown in photo 4-31, take standard shafting epoxy and, using a mixing stick, apply the epoxy to the cork.

Drop the cork into the butt end of the shaft. Be sure the tapered end of the cork goes in first (see photo 4-32).

Using a 45-inch Ram Rod (Stock #864), push the cork down the shaft as far as it will go (see photo 4-33). Do not jam the rod in as hard as you can. Use a smooth firm pressure to get the cork to the bottom or tip of the

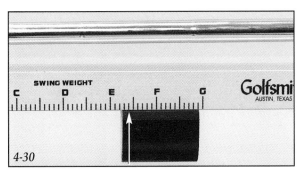

4-30

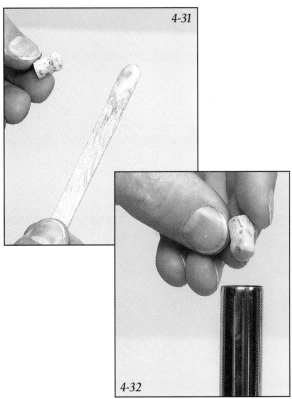

4-31

4-32

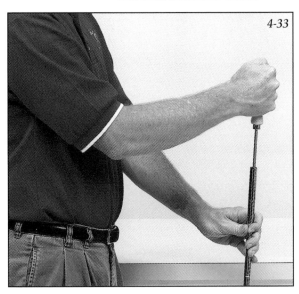

4-33

4-34

4-35

4-36

4-37

shaft, then a couple of firm taps should do. This will set the cork in the proper place.

There will usually be some lead powder that remains loose in the shaft after the cork is installed. You want to remove this from the shaft. Simply turn the shaft but down and tap firmly on a hard surface. The powder residue should all come out the butt of the shaft (see photo 4-34).

It is important to be sure the cork is as far down the shaft as possible. To do this, place the Ram Rod down the shaft until it stops. Using your thumb (you can mark the rod with a marker), mark the depth of the rod. This is easiest to do if the club is placed in a vice as shown in photo 4-35.

Remove the rod from the shaft and place it along side the shaft, noting the point you have marked as being the depth of the cork. The rod should indicate the powder and cork is at least down to the top of the hosel, and preferably as low into the head as possible. This will vary, depending on how much weight is added (see photo 4-36). If the rod stops well above the ferrule, it is likely that the cork did not get all the way down into the proper position. If this occurs, take the rod and attempt to ram the cork further down the shaft, then repeat the procedures described above and shown in 4-35, and 4-36.

Install the grip (see photo 4-37). For complete gripping instructions, see Chapter 2.

Recheck the swingweight (see photo 4-38). Note the reading in this example is D4.

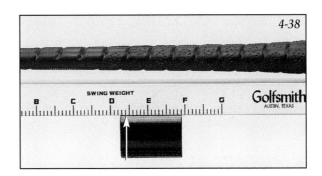

4-38

GRAPHITE SHAFTS

Graphite shafts in irons have not been as popular as they have in woods, but they have come a long way in the last few years. While a majority of the touring professionals still use steel, advances in graphite iron shafts have given the professionals, and amateurs alike, many more and better options. One of the biggest advantages in using graphite in irons is the reduction in the overall weight of the club. For amateurs, this can really give them a big advantage over steel-shafted irons. The less physically strong the player, the bigger the advantage. Let's face it, lighter clubs are easier to swing than heavy clubs are, and therein lies the advantage. Graphite also has a natural shock-absorbing component that does dampen the vibration of impact. This can be a help for those people with joint ailments (there are steel shafts with special designs and inserts that can also reduce the shock of impact).

The procedures for shafting irons and wedges with graphite are very similar to those used for shafting metal woods. Even if you are familiar with the procedures, please read through all of them before you begin. Do not take any short cuts. It is very important to follow the instructions, step by step, to ensure proper assembly. If you have any questions, or do not understand any of the procedures on the following pages, please contact Golfsmith for assistance.

One of the biggest advantages in using graphite in irons is the reduction in the overall weight of the club.

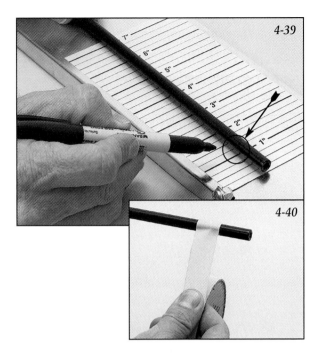

4-39

4-40

If the shaft you choose calls for the tip to be trimmed for flex, first measure the proper amount to trim from the tip and mark the shaft (see photo 4-39).

To protect the graphite shaft from splitting or splintering when it is cut, take a piece of ¾-inch masking tape and tape the shaft just above the mark where the shaft is to be cut (see photo 4-40). The tape should actually be touching the mark. You can actually tape the shaft first, then mark the shaft. You can put the mark right on the tape. This will make the mark a little easier to see, especially on black shafts. Then simply cut the shaft on the mark.

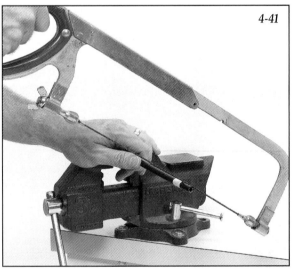

4-41

There are, as with steel, several methods of cutting graphite. **NOTE:** *DO NOT USE the Stock #858 Shaft Cutter. It is designed for steel shafts only.* Photo 4-41 shows the Stock #8586 Rod Saw Blade. When attached to a standard hack saw this blade cuts graphite cleanly and quickly. Place the shaft in a vice. It is recommended to use the Stock #8288-Small Metal Vise Clamp to protect the shaft in the vise. To cut the shaft, place the blade on the mark and using a normal sawing motion, cut the tip of the shaft as shown. An alternative blade to use is the Stock #8587 Grit–Edge Saw Blade.

4-42

An alternative to using the hacksaw is the Cutoff Wheel (Stock #8581). This wheel attaches to a bench grinder or electric motor and cuts graphite, as well as steel. This wheel should be used with at least ⅓ h.p. motors. Photo 4-42 shows the positioning of the shaft when cutting. Simply place the shaft against the wheel and apply slight pressure. The blade will cut the shaft quickly and evenly. As always, be sure to wear safety glasses when using any kind of power equipment.

After trimming the tip of the shaft, you must prepare the tip surface for insertion into the head. Some graphite shafts are painted all the way to the tip of the shaft and others have approximately one inch of the tip unfinished from the factory. In both, cases you still have to rough up the surface of the tip. Be sure you know what the bore depth of the head will be before you begin prepping the tip. Measure the bore depth using a pencil or similar object and mark the shaft accordingly (see *SPECIAL NOTE* and Diagram 3-1 on page 29 for important details on this procedure). If the shaft fits into the head easily, you can insert the shaft and mark the shaft at the top of the hosel. Do not force the shaft into the head. You may want to tape off the shaft just above the area to be prepped (see photo 4–43a). This protects the shaft from scratching or marking above the hosel line. Photo 4-43 shows one technique for preparing the tip of a graphite shaft. A knife can be used for scraping the tip of the shaft. You only want to rough up the amount of the tip that will be in the hosel. Using the knife, position as shown and lightly scrape the tip. You just want to remove the finish from the tip, or lightly scrape the tip of the shaft on those that do not have the finish on them (see photo 4-43b for view of tip after scraping).

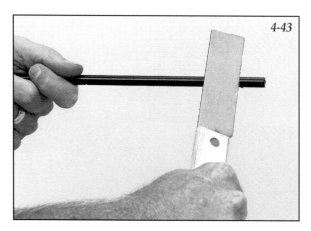

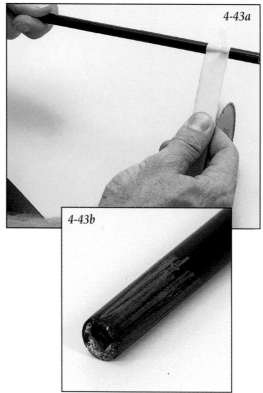

DO NOT cut into the fibers of the graphite. After scrapping the shaft, wipe the tip off with a damp cloth to remove any residue.

Another method is to use Surface Conditioning Strips (Stock #4875). The procedure is much the same as using sand paper on steel shafts. Place the shaft in a vice, being sure to use a Rubber Vice Clamp to protect the shaft. On graphite shafts, Stock #8288 is recommended. Take the strip, as shown in photo 4-44 and work the strip back and forth over the tip of the shaft. Again, tape the shaft above the hosel line to prevent from prepping too far up the shaft. Be sure to rotate the shaft to ensure the entire circumference of the tip is prepped.

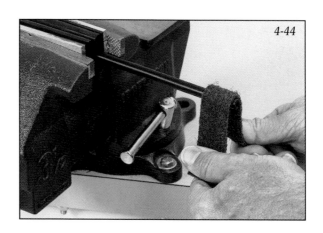

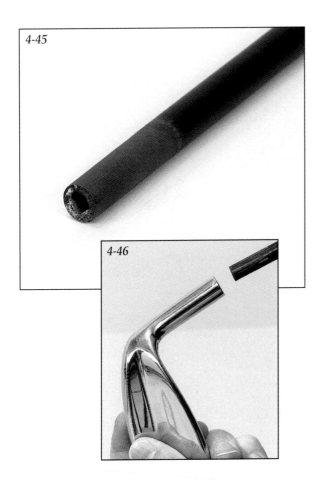

4-45

4-46

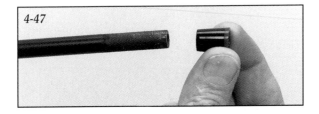

4-47

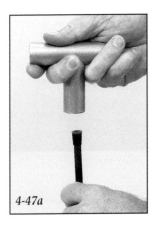

4-47a

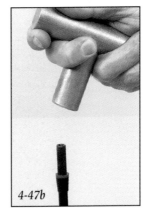

4-47b

After preparing the tip, wipe it off with a clean damp cloth to remove any dust left on the tip. Photo 4–45 shows a close up view of the shaft tip after using the surface-conditioning belt.

Test fit the shaft into the head (see photo 4-46). Be sure the shaft goes in all the way to the bottom of the bore. The shaft should already be marked to indicate the bore depth. If not, or if the mark is no longer on the shaft, measure the depth of the hosel and mark the shaft.

If the head requires a ferrule, place the ferrule on to the shaft. The ferrule can be installed onto the shaft prior to epoxying the head in place or at the time the head is installed. To install the ferrule without epoxy, first place the ferrule over the tip of the shaft (see photo 4-47). A tool you can use to help with the installation of ferrules is the Mr. T Ferrule Installer (Stock #8296). After placing the ferrule over the tip of the shaft, use the installer to drive the ferrule on, approximately one inch onto the shaft (see photos 4-47a and 4-47b). The ferrule will be driven the remainder of the way on the shaft by using the head (see photo 4-49).

Another ferrule installation tool you can use is the Stock #351 Ferrule Installation Tool. To use, check the bore depth with the knurled rod (see photo 4-48) and then set the rod in place by tightening the round handle. Next, turn the tool around and with a light tapping motion tap the ferrule onto the shaft (see photo 4-48a). This puts the ferrule at the precise point of full hosel penetration. See **SPECIAL NOTE** and Diagram 3-3 on page 47 for additional instructions.

The head can actually be used to install the ferrule to its full penetration. Once the ferrule has been partially installed, simply take the head and use it as the driving tool to put the ferrule in exactly the right place. Holding the shaft firmly in one hand and the head in the other (see photo 4-49), firmly tap the butt of the shaft on a hard surface. This will drive the shaft through the ferrule and to the bottom of the bore. NOTE: An alternative method is to install the ferrule at the time the head is being epoxied to the shaft. To do this, simply dip the tip of the shaft into the epoxy mix. Slide the ferrule over the shaft tip. You can then drive the ferrule on with the head as shown in photo 4-49. The head should then be removed and the proper amount of epoxy should be applied to the shaft tip and the hosel of the head.

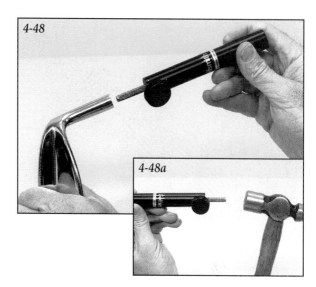

4-48

4-48a

Its time to mark the shaft for final length cutting. First place the head on the shaft dry (with no epoxy). Be sure the head is all the way on. Since the ferrule is now pre-set on the shaft, you can tell easily when the head is all the way on the shaft. If the head will not stay on, you can place a small piece of tape on the tip of the shaft to provide a snug fit for the measuring process. You must be sure the head is on properly or the length cut might be affected. Photo 4-50 and 4-51 show two methods for measuring the shaft for cutting to final length. The True Measure Precision Club Rule (Stock #4606) works well on your bench or tabletop (photo 4-50). Note the mark on the shaft is approximately ⅛ inch below the desired final club length. In this example the desired final club length is 36 inches. Cutting the shaft ⅛ inch to ¼ inch below the desired final club length allows for the extra length added by the grip butt cap when the grip is installed.

4-49

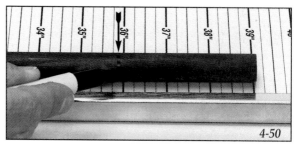

4-50

The 48-inch Combination Ruler is used by putting the club in the playing position and marking the shaft for the length cut (see photo 4-51). Again, note the position of the mark on the shaft to allow for the grip gap.

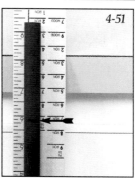

4-51

4-52

4-52a

4-53

Photo 4-52 shows the Stock #8586 Rod Saw Blade on a standard hack saw being used to cut the graphite shaft to length. The Stock #8587 Grit–Edge Saw Blade can also be used. Place the shaft in a vise, being sure to use a shaft protecting vise clamp (Stock #8248 for shaft butts is shown) to prevent damage to the shaft in the vise. Once the shaft is securely in the vise, place the saw blade on the mark, and with a normal to slow sawing motion, cut the shaft. Photo 4-52a illustrates the use of the Stock #8581 6-inch cutoff wheel on a standard bench type grinder being used to cut the butt of a graphite shaft. Simply position the shaft as shown and apply slight pressure to the blade to cut the shaft. A ⅓ hp motor is the minimum power that can be used with this cutoff wheel. **NOTE:** *Always remember to wear protective eyewear when using power equipment.*

Photo 4-53 shows a close up view of the shaft after cutting. Note the length is approximately ⅛ inch under our desired final club length. As mentioned earlier, the cap end of the grip will make this up once the grip is installed.

The final step before the actual assembly process begins is to check to see what the swingweight of the club will be. To do this, you will need an old grip that you can split. The grip should be the same kind that will be used in the final assembly process, or at least one that is the same weight as the grip that will be used in the final assembly. This easily slips over the butt of the shaft. The purpose is to simulate what the final swingweight will be after assembly and to determine if any weight will need to be added during the assembly process. The head should be placed on the tip end of the shaft dry (with no epoxy), making sure the shaft goes in the head to the bottom of the bore. Since the ferrule is pre-set, you can tell when the head is on properly.

Now, check the swingweight reading (see photo 4-54). In this example note the swingweight is approximately D6. **NOTE:** *Measuring the swingweight of a golf club prior to and after assembly is not required in the assembly process. For a definition of swingweight and its function, refer to the Appendix and the Glossary of clubmaking terms. Golfsmith sells several swingweight scale models.*

Before you can epoxy the shaft into the head, you must clean out the hosel. This is necessary to clean out any dirt, oil, etc. that may have been left in the hosel during the manufacturing process. The first recommended step is to use a Hosel Cleaning Brush (Stock #8625). As illustrated in photo 4-55, the silicon carbide bristles on the flex hone tool are pushed into the hosel with a twisting motion. This will remove or loosen unwanted material in the hosel. It also roughs up the inside of the hosel, which aids in the adhesion process. The next step is to take cotton swabs (see photo 4 –55a), dip them into some acetone and swab out the hosel. This will clean out the remaining residue. Once you have swabbed out the hosel with acetone, set it aside to dry for a few minutes. **NOTE:** *This is a very important step. Many epoxy bond failures are due to contaminants in the epoxy that come from the hosel.*

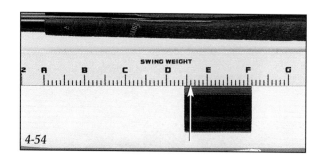

4-54

There are several models of swing-weight scales in the Golfsmith Components Catalog.

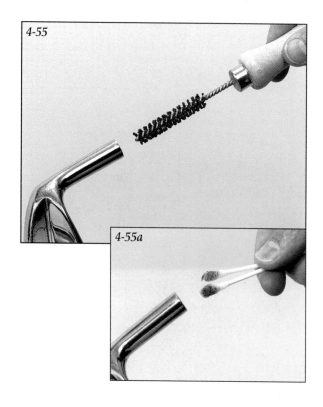

4-55

4-55a

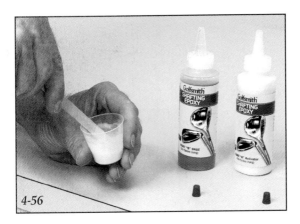

4-56

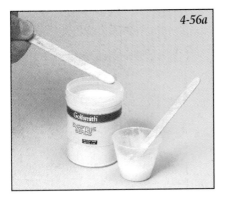

4-56a

It is best to use mixing cups similar to the one pictured.

SPECIAL NOTE:

All of the heads in the Golfsmith catalog have been designed with a special "coning" or beveling on the inside top of the hosel. This is necessary to prevent premature graphite shaft failure caused by a sharp edge against a graphite shaft at the top of the hosel. If you are using a head that is not coned, and are shafting with a graphite shaft, you will have to cone or bevel the top of the hosel. This requires a use of a 20-degree Countersink (Stock #794) bit in a hand drill. After the coning operation is done, a Round Ball Deburrer (Stock #793) can be used to smooth out the burrs caused by the coning operation. This is only necessary on heads that have not been, or have insufficient coning when they are going to be shafted with a graphite shaft.

It's time to epoxy the head onto the shaft. There are two types of epoxy that can be used equally well with graphite shafts. The Golfsmith Graphite Shafting Epoxy (Stock #995 for 10 oz. quantity) or the Golfsmith Standard Shafting Epoxy (Stock #9095 for half-pint size). It is best to use mixing cups similar to the one pictured. The Graphite shafting epoxy, Stock #995, mixes 2 parts activator (Part A) to 3 parts base (Part B). If using this epoxy, simply pour out the proper amounts of Part A and Part B in separate cups, then mix together (see photo 4-56). If using the Stock #9095 Standard Golfsmith Epoxy, simply pour out equal amounts of Part A and Part B into separate cups (mixes to a 1 to 1 ratio), then mix together. It is very important to mix thoroughly. Mix for at least one minute. Mix until the epoxy is a consistent color throughout. Photo inset 4-56a shows a product called epoxy beads. They are tiny glass beads that can be added to epoxy for to insure adequate epoxy cushion between the shaft and hosel wall. These beads can reduce the possibility of shafting a club off-center. If the shaft is a loose fit in the hosel, we recommend using these beads (Stock #9082). If the shaft is a good fit and does not lean when put into the hosel, the beads are not necessary.

If weight needs to be added for swingweighting purposes, there are a couple of methods to consider. Photo 4-57 shows a graphite shaft tip weight. These weights come in a variety of weights (two grams to five grams, see inset 4-57a) and are available in the Golfsmith Components Catalog. These weights are installed at the time of assembly and after dipping the stem in the epoxy simply slip into the tip of the shaft.

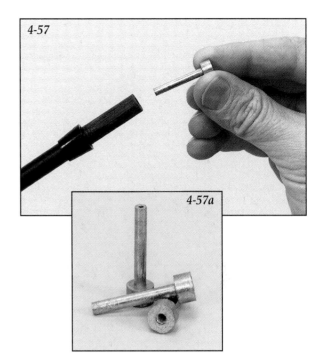

In some cases, depending on the type of graphite shaft, the shaft tip weights may not fit into the tip of the shaft. In those cases, you can use a small drill bit (⅛ inch) and ream out the tip of the shaft. You must be very careful not to damage the fibers of the shaft. In photo 4-58, the shaft has been secured into a vise using a protective shaft clamp (Stock #8249). Using a standard hand drill and a ⅛-inch drill bit, slowly ream out the tip of the shaft. Only go into the shaft the amount necessary to allow the tip weight proper penetration.

After reaming the tip of the shaft, test fit the tip weight (see photo 4-59).

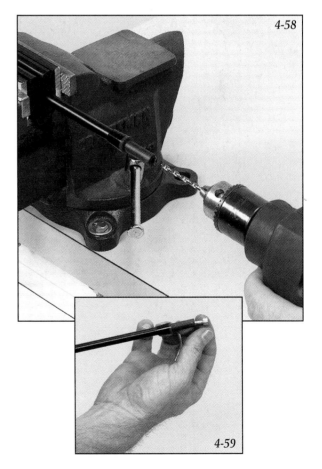

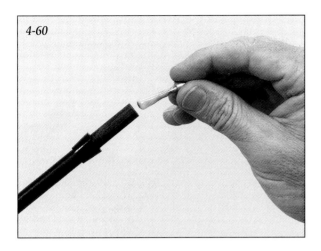

4-60

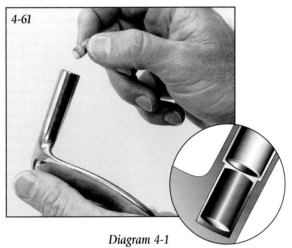

4-61

Diagram 4-1
Proper Position of Hosel Bore Weight in Head.

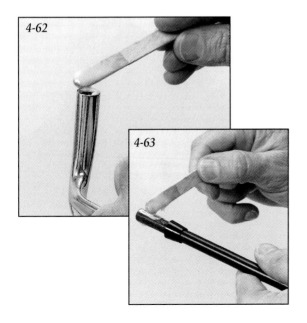

4-62

4-63

When you're ready to assemble the clubhead, dip the weight into the epoxy and insert the weight into the tip of the shaft (see photo 4-60).

SPECIAL NOTE:
As photo 4-57 on page 83 shows, these shaft tip weights have a head on them that will add approximately ¼ inch to the length of the club. Because of this, it will be necessary to trim that amount from the tip of the shaft. Follow the same procedures as you did when trimming the tip before, taping the area to be cut and using either the hacksaw with the rod saw blade in the photo, or with a cut off wheel. It is also possible to simply grind or file the tip. A 30- or 42-inch belt sander with a medium grit belt will also do the trick. Whichever method you use, the shaft tip should be taped with masking tape to prevent damage to the graphite fibers.

Many of the heads in the Golfsmith Components Catalog feature a hosel weight port, which allows a special lead or tungsten weight plug to be installed into the bottom of the hosel. As with the shaft tip weights, this allows for increasing the swingweight at the time of assembly. To install, simply coat the weight in epoxy and drop in the hosel (see photo 4-61). Be sure the weight falls all the way to the bottom of the weight port (see Diagram 4-1).

It's time to install the shaft. Using a mixing stick, put a small bead of epoxy on the inside of the hosel (see photo 4-62). Do not fill the hosel. A small amount is all that is necessary.

Next, take the mixing stick and coat the outside of the tip of the shaft with epoxy (see photo 4-63). Be sure to get a good coverage over the tip of the shaft.

One option, instead of using the mixing stick, is to simply dip the shaft tip into the epoxy mix as shown in photo 4-64. Again, be sure you get good coverage on the outside of the shaft tip.

SPECIAL NOTE: *In some cases, shimming the shaft tip is necessary to secure a good fit.*

Photo inset 4-64a shows the Stock number 8275 Oversize bore shaft shims. These are used when the hosel is too big for the shaft. The shims come in three sizes and are placed on the shaft just prior to applying the epoxy (see photo 4-64b). Photo 4-64c shows a mesh dry wall tape that is sold at local hardware stores that can also be used. Again, this tape is applied just prior to applying the epoxy. Only shim the tip of a shaft if the shaft will not stay perfectly centered or straight in the head. Shafting beads can also be used.

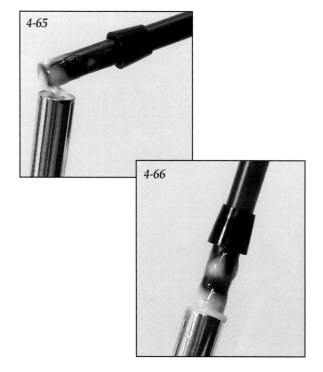

Once the shaft tip is thoroughly coated, you can use it to spread the epoxy on the inside of the hosel (see photo 4-65).

Install the shaft by inserting it into the hosel, slowly rotating or twisting the shaft as it goes into the hosel (see photo 4-66). Once you have the shaft all the in the hosel, pull the shaft about half way out, still rotating it, and re-insert the shaft all the way. This insures that epoxy is covering every area inside the hosel and on the shaft tip.

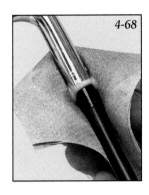

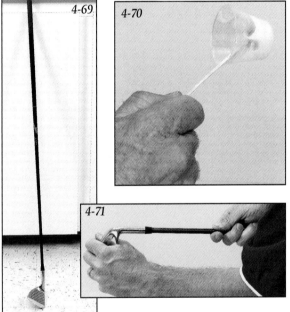

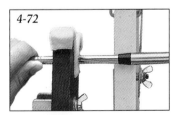

Turn the club upside down and gently tap the butt of the shaft on a hard surface (see photo 4-67). This helps insure the shaft is inserted all the way to the bottom of the hosel.

Using a paper towel dampened with solvent, wipe the excess epoxy off of the hosel and ferrule area (see photo 4-68). It is much easier to wipe this area clean when the epoxy is still wet, so be meticulous. Get it as clean as possible.

Set the club aside, with the head down, to cure. (see photo 4-69).

After the proper cure time has past, first check the epoxy mix left in the cup (see photo 4-70).

Check the head for tightness (see photo 4-71).

If the club you have assembled has a ferrule, the ferrule portion of the club may need finishing or cleaning up after the assembly is complete. Most ferrules will be slightly larger than outside diameter of the hosel. To get a clean, professional look, it is recommended that the ferrule be "turned down" or smoothed so it is the same diameter of the hosel. This can be done using a linen polishing belt on a 30- or 42-inch belt sander. If you use a 30- or 42-inch belt sander, we recommend you practice on a few old clubs before you start. Photo 4-72, shows the Stock #8209 Ferrule Turning Support Arm with a 42-inch belt sander with motor. If a belt sander is not available the ferrule can be turned down by hand. Use masking tape to cover the shaft and hosel. Sand the ferrule down, using a file and/or a fine grit sand paper. In most cases, the ferrule is very close to size of the outside diameter of the hosel. In these cases, you can simply take a cotton swabs or a clean cloth dampened with acetone and rub it over the ferrule evenly. This gives the ferrule a nice, clean, glossy shine (see photo 4-72b).

Check the swingweight using a split grip. If you have added weight during the assembly process by using the shaft tip inserts or the hosel weight inserts, this will give you a close approximation of what the final swingweight will be when the club is gripped. If you did not add weight during the assembly process and you find that you would like to add a little more weight to increase the swingweight, you still can. In this example, photo 4-73 indicates that the swingweight is D6. If this is the desired swingweight, all that is left is to grip the club (see photo 4-81). If you want to add more weight, go to photo 4-74 (Refer to important *NOTE:* on SensiCore, page 72). It is not recommended that this be done in addition to shaft tip weights or hosel weight port weights. This should be done as an alternative method. The inside diameters of some graphite shafts may be too small, not allowing the weight of the cork to be installed in the proper position. Also if the club is being made to final club length longer than 46 inches, the Ram Rod may not go to the bottom of the shaft. As a test, you should place a Ram Rod down the graphite to see how far down additional lead or tungstun powder and a cork will go. If it does not go to the depth required, do not use this method.

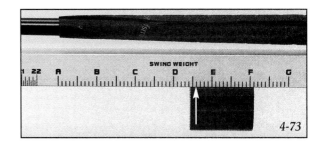

4-73

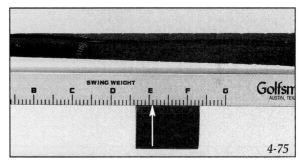

4-74

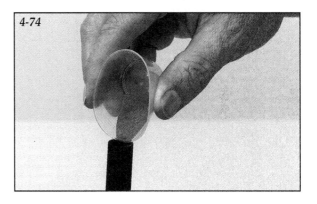

4-75

To add more weight, measure out the amount of lead powder (Stock #942) you want to add and pour it down the shaft. Two grams equals approximately one swingweight point. Once you have poured the lead powder into the butt end of the shaft (see photo 4-74), tap the club gently against a hard surface to insure the powder is all the way to the bottom of the shaft. It is recommended that no more than eight to 10 grams be added down the shaft using this method. More than that amount could effect the playability of the club.

Recheck the swingweight with the split grip. Note in the example (photo 4-75) the swingweight is now D8.

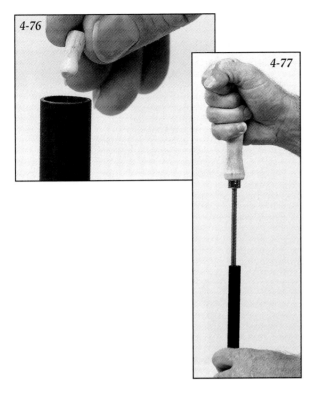

Once the desired amount of weight is added, a cork must be epoxied down the shaft to prevent the lead powder from coming out. There are different types for corks for different types of shafts. Graphite iron shafts require Stock #882C in the Golfsmith Components Catalog. Apply regular shafting epoxy to the cork and drop it into the butt end of the shaft. Be sure to drop the tapered end of the cork into the shaft first (see photo 4-76).

Using a Ram Rod for Graphite Shafts (Stock #8645), firmly push the cork down to the tip end of the shaft. Remove the rod from the shaft (see photo 4-77).

There will usually be some lead powder that remains loose in the shaft after the cork is installed. You want to remove this from the shaft. Simply turn the shaft butt down and tap firmly on a hard surface. All of the powder residue should come out the butt end of the shaft (see photo 4-78).

It is important to make sure that the cork is in the proper place inside the shaft. To check the corks position, put the Ram Rod back into the shaft as far down as it will go. Mark the shaft with a marker or you thumb (see photo 4-79) and remove the rod.

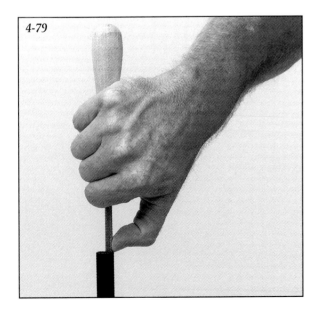

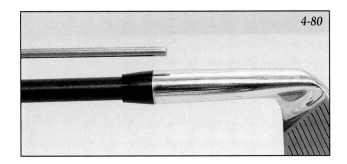
4-80

Place the rod along side the outside of the club and check the depth. Photo 4-80 shows a close up of the rod tip and the approximate depth the cork is in the shaft. It is not recommended that the cork be above the hosel line. Any epoxy or epoxied piece of material inside the shaft that is above the hosel line could cause the shaft to prematurely fail.

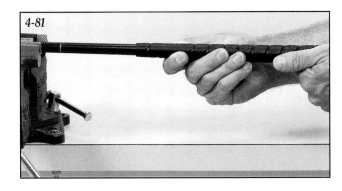
4-81

Install the grip (see photo 4-81). For complete gripping instructions, see Chapter 2.

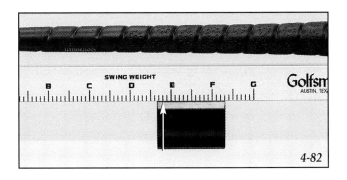
4-82

Re-check the swingweight. In this example, the final swingweight is D8 (see photo 4-82).

Items Needed for Metal Wood Assembly:

❑ Golf Club Components – heads, shafts, grips, ferrules *(if necessary)*

❑ Organic Grip Solvent

❑ ¾-inch or 2-inch, two-sided tape

❑ Shafting Epoxy

❑ Mixing Cups and Sticks

❑ Shaft Cutting Tools

   Stock #858- Shaft Cutter or Stock #8581- Cutoff Wheel for steel shafts

   Stock #'s- 8587, 8586 Saw Blades or Stock #8581- Cutoff Wheel for graphite shafts

❑ Vise Clamps

   Stock #8248 for shaft butts, Stock #8249 for shaft tips and general use

❑ 48-Inch Combination Ruler – Stock #8460 or Precision Golf Club Rule – Stock #4606

❑ Coarse grit sandpaper for prepping steel shafts, surface conditioning belt for graphite shafts

❑ Knife for prepping graphite shafts

❑ Flex Hone Tool for cleaning hosels, Stock #8625 for irons, Stock #86255w for woods

❑ Cotton Swabs - Acetone

❑ Bench Vise

❑ 30-inch or 42-inch Belt Sander for use in shaft prepping of steel and Graphite shafts - *optional*

❑ Mr. T Ferrule Installer, Stock #8296 or Ferrule Installation Tool, Stock #351 - *optional*

❑ Swingweight Scale - *optional*

❑ Shaft tip weights for steel and graphite shafts, hosel weight port weights - *optional*

❑ Tungsten Powder- Stock #9466 and corks- Stock #882 A, C - *optional*

❑ Epoxy Beads, Stock #9082 - *optional*

❑ Split grip for swingweighting purposes - *optional*

Chapter 5
Making Putters

Many times, the first club a person builds for themselves is a putter. In fact, the putter and the driver are the two most popular clubs people assemble. Obviously, most of these golfers are looking for that little magic that might help them drive the ball farther or make more putts. Putters can be the best choice when attempting clubmaking for the first time. Many of the techniques and procedures used and learned while making a putter will carry over to other club assembly projects.

Why build a putter? Consider the number of times you use a putter in a round of golf. Consider the number of times you use other clubs, like a driver or a wedge. You use the putter far more than the other clubs in your bag, therefore, the positive impact on your game could be substantial. Not to mention the fact that putters are fun and inexpensive to make. The next time you are in a pro shop look at the prices of some the name brand putters and compare that to what it costs to buy the components and put together your own putter and you will see what we mean. Also, there is quite a bit of satisfaction that comes with building your own club. You may find that once you build your first putter and play with it, your playing partners may want you to build them one too.

The first step to building your putter is selecting the head. Golfsmith carries many different putter head models in the Components Catalog. Blade-style, cavity-back, heel-toe weighted and mallet are just some of the models available from Golfsmith. Materials used include brass, stainless, nickel and aluminum. There are combinations of materials used in some designs to enhance perimeter weighting. Face insert materials made of rubber, special polymers and copper are popular in putters and can enhance or change feel. Knowing which one is the right one for you and your game is largely a cosmetic decision. However, it is important to know that certain styles of putters can offer some performance benefits. Any style of putter that is designed with perimeter or peripheral weighting is more forgiving on off-center hits than those that are not. Be sure to examine the putters you are considering, noting the material the putter is made from and design features, along with the look.

After you have choose the putter head, shaft and grip selections come next. In the shaft selection, be sure the shaft is compatible with the head. All of the putter models carried by Golfsmith have either a .370" hosel bore or are of the over hosel variety. Also, note the putter head styles that require a bent putter shaft and match accordingly. The assembly of all of these putter heads and shafts are covered in this chapter.

The grip selection is largely a feel issue. You want the size and texture of the grip to feel comfortable in your hands. Again, there is wide variety of putter grips available. Go with what feels best in your hands or the hands of the player you are building the putter for.

Once the selection process is complete, your almost ready. We suggest that you review all of the procedures in this chapter before you start to assemble your putter. If this is your first time, reviewing the procedures before hand may help prevent mistakes. We suggest a dry run, following the procedures pictured with the various components in hand. Once you understand the procedures, mix your epoxy and do the final assembly. Do not skip any of the

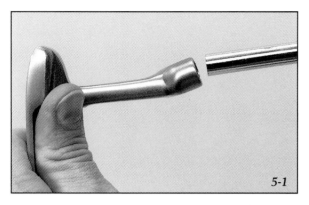

5-1

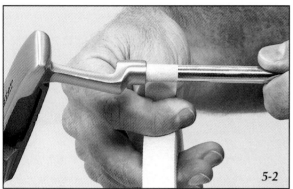

5-2

5-3

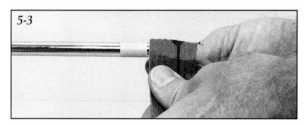

5-3a

5-3b

5-3c

steps outlined. They are there for a reason. By following the steps outlined, you will find that the actual assembly of a putter is a breeze.

IN – HOSEL DESIGN

The next step to assembling your putter once you have chosen the components is to test fit the shaft into the hosel (see photo 5-1). Check the bore depth of the hosel with a pencil and note the measurement of the depth for reference. In some cases, it may be necessary to prep the tip of the shaft or remove the chrome from the tip of the shaft first so it slips into the head (see photo 5 -3a,b,c for different methods of preparing the shaft. Procedures for all three methods will follow). In some rare cases, it may be necessary to ream the hosel of the putter head slightly to get the shaft to fit. To do this, simply take a ⅜-inch drill bit and using a hand drill, ream out the hosel.

Once the shaft is in the hosel, take ¾-inch masking tape and tape around the shaft right up to the top of the hosel (see photo 5-2). This marks the shaft for the proper installation depth and protects the shaft during the tip abrading process from scratching above the hosel line.

Now remove the shaft from the head, and abrade the tip of the shaft. Photo 5-3 shows this process using a medium to coarse grit sandpaper, cut in a one-inch strip, being used to rough up the tip of the steel shaft. Place the shaft in a vise using a protective rubber vise clamp (Stock #913 or Stock #8249) and abrade the tip, being careful not to tear the tape. Photo 5-3a shows the procedure using a fine tooth file. Photo 5-3b shows the procedure using a 30-inch belt sander (a 42-inch belt sander can also be used) and a medium to coarse grit sanding belt. Whichever method you use, be sure to abrade the entire circumference of the shaft tip. Photo 5-3c shows a close up view of how the shaft tip should look after this procedure is completed.

Re-check the shaft fit in the head (see photo 5-4).

With the putter head on the shaft, measure the shaft for final length. To do this, put the club in its playing position and measure using a 48-inch Combination Ruler (Stock #8460). Lay the ruler behind the shaft and mark the shaft for the desired final length. Photo 5-5 shows the shaft marked just below the 35 inch mark. This will give a final putter length when assembled with a grip of 35 inches. When marking the shaft for the final length cut, always allow ⅛ inch to ¼ inch for the grip butt cap. In this case the shaft is actually cut to 34 ⅞ inches.

Remove the head from the shaft and cut the shaft to length. Photo 5-6 shows cutting the shaft using the Stock #858 Super Shaft Cutter. The shaft can also be cut with a 6-inch cutoff wheel (Stock #8581) on at least a ⅓ h.p. motor. See page 33 in photo 3-11b for illustration.

With the head on the shaft, re-check the length. Photo 5-7 shows the final cut shaft length at 34⅞ inches.

Before you can epoxy the shaft into the head, you must clean out the hosel. This is necessary to clean out any dirt, oil, etc. that may have been left in the hosel during the manufacturing process. The first recommended step is to use a Flex Hone Tool (Stock #8625). As illustrated in photo 5-8, the silicon carbide bristles on the Flex Hone Tool are pushed into the hosel with a twisting motion. This removes or loosens unwanted material in the hosel. It also roughs up the inside of the hosel, which aids in the adhesion process. The next step is to take some cotton swabs (see photo 5-8a), dip them into acetone and swab out the hosel. This cleans out all remaining residue. Once you have swabbed out the hosel with acetone, set it aside to dry for a few minutes. *NOTE: This is a very important step. Many epoxy bond failures are due to contaminants in the epoxy that come from the hosel.*

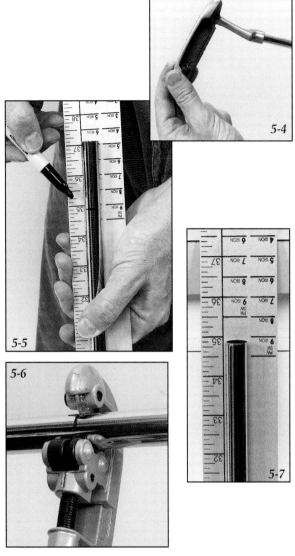

5-4

5-5

5-6

5-7

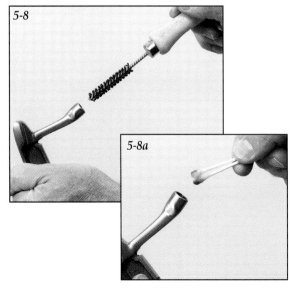

5-8

5-8a

5-9

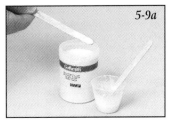

5-9a

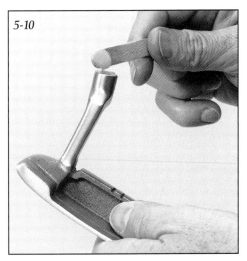

5-10

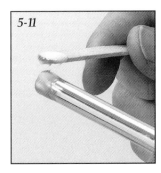

5-11

5-12

It's time to epoxy the head onto the shaft. We recommend using the Golfsmith Shafting Epoxy (Stock #9095 for half pint quantity). Parts A and B mix at a 1 : 1 ratio. It is best to use mixing cups similar to the one pictured. Simply pour out equal amounts of Part A and Part B in separate cups, then mix together. It is very important to mix thoroughly. Mix for at least one minute. Mix until the epoxy is a consistent color throughout (see photo 5-9). Photo 5-9a shows a product called epoxy beads. They are tiny glass beads that can be added to epoxy to insure adequate epoxy cushion between the shaft and hosel wall. These beads can eliminate the possibility of shafting a club off-center. If the shaft is a loose fit in the hosel, we recommend using these beads (Stock #9082). If the shaft is a good fit and does not lean when put into the hosel, the beads are not necessary.

Now install the shaft. Using a mixing stick, put a small bead of epoxy on the inside of the hosel (see photo 5-10). Do not fill the hosel. A small amount is all that is necessary.

Next, take the mixing stick and coat the outside of the tip of the shaft with epoxy (see photo 5-11). Be sure to get a good coverage over the tip of the shaft.

One option, instead of using the mixing stick, is to simply dip the shaft tip into the epoxy mix as shown in photo 5-12. Again, be sure you get good coverage on the outside of the shaft tip.

Once the shaft tip is thoroughly coated, you can use it to spread the epoxy on the inside of the hosel (see photo 5-13).

5-13

Install the shaft by inserting it into the hosel, slowly rotating or twisting the shaft as it goes into the hosel (see photo 5-14). Once you have the shaft all the way in the hosel, pull the shaft about half way out, still rotating it, and re-insert the shaft all the way. This helps to insure that epoxy is covering every area inside the hosel and on the shaft tip.

5-14

Turn the club upside down and gently tap the butt of the shaft on a hard surface (see photo 5-15). Do not tap the butt on vinyl, wood or tile floors. A concrete floor, metal block or scrap wood block is recommended. This helps insure the shaft is inserted all the way to the bottom of the hosel.

5-15

Using a paper towel, wipe the excess epoxy from around the top of the bore or hosel and off of the shaft (see photo 5-16). It helps to dampen the towel with an organic grip solvent. Wipe as much of the excess epoxy off as possible. You should be able to get it completely clean. It is much easier to get this area clean when the epoxy is wet, so be meticulous.

5-16

5-17

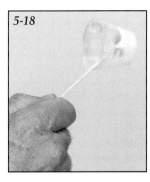

5-18

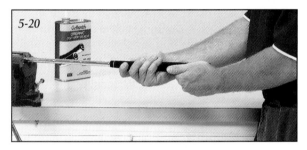

5-19

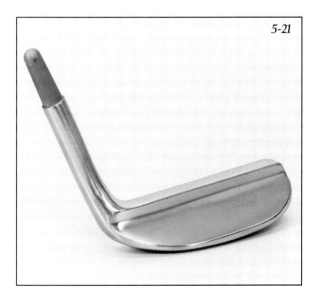

5-20

Set the club aside to cure in a secure place with the head down (see photo 5-17).

After the appropriate time for curing has past (approximately 24 hours), check the mixing cup to see if the mix used for the club has cured (see photo 5-18). If the epoxy in the cup appears soft and not cured, do not use the club. Cure rates can vary depending on the outside temperature. At room temperature, 24 hours should be sufficient. Most shafting epoxies will be very hard when they cure. If the epoxy is cured correctly, it should appear hard and if pressed firmly with a mixing stick, should leave little, if any indentation. See *SPECIAL NOTE:* on page 38 for more information on epoxy.

Check the head for tightness (see photo 5-19).

Install the grip (see photo 5-20). For complete instructions on installing grips, see Chapter 2.

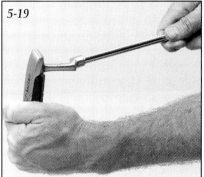

5-21

OVER HOSEL DESIGN

Another style of putter you can assemble requires the shaft to be attached over the hosel stem of the head (see photo 5-21). Some of these models will use a specially designed over-the-hosel shaft. In the example illustrated here, a special flared tip steel shaft is used that is designed for this over-the-hosel style putter. Again, it is very important that you follow the procedures step by step. For your reference, the head model in the illustration is the Harvey Penick Red River model (Stock #P4300) from the Harvey Penick Components Catalog and the shaft is the Stock #270 Flared Tip Steel Putter Shaft in the Golfsmith Components Catalog.

Using the Flex Hone Tool (Stock #7505) or similar type wire brush tool, clean out the inside of the flared tip portion of the shaft (see photo 5-22). After using the brush, take a cotton swab and solvent and swab out the inside of the flared shaft tip portion of the shaft. You can see in photo inset 5-22a the residue that must be cleaned out to insure a good epoxy bond.

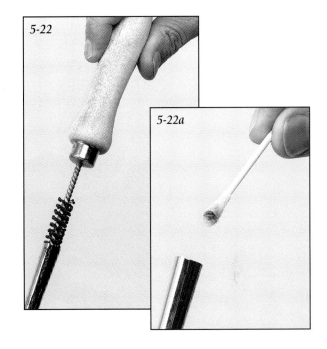

It is also necessary to abrade or rough up the surface of the stem on the head that will be going inside the shaft. Place the head in a vise as shown in photo 5-23. Be sure to use vise pads (Stock #8936 are shown) to protect the finish of the head. Using a medium or coarse grit one inch strip of sandpaper, rough up the stem. Be careful not to scratch the hosel of the head below the stem. A few wraps of masking tape around the hosel below the stem will help prevent any scratches in as of a slight mishap. (not pictured) Photo 5-23a illustrates the same procedure using a fine to medium cut file. Do not take too much of the material off of the stem. All you are trying to do is slightly rough up the surface to aid the epoxy bond. Photo 5-23b shows the same procedure using a 30-inch belt sander with a coarse grit sanding belt. A 30-inch or 42-inch belt sander can be used. Be sure to wear protective goggles when using a belt sander, or any type of power equipment.

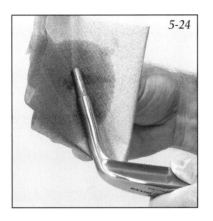

5-24

After you have roughed up the stem of the putter head, take a paper towel or cloth damp with solvent and wipe off the stem (see photo 5-24). The abrading process leaves residue on the stem that can contaminate the epoxy. It is very important to remove this residue from the stem of the putter head.

Photo 5-25 shows a close up view of the putter head stem after the abrading and cleaning process.

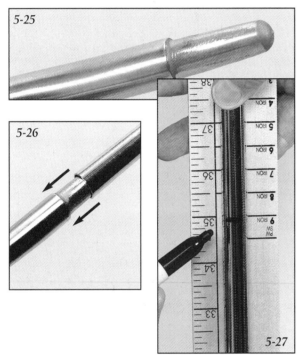

5-25

5-26

5-27

Test fit the shaft on the head. The shaft should slip over the stem and flush up to the top of the hosel, leaving no gaps (see photo 5-26).

With the head on the shaft, place the putter in the playing position. Place the 48-inch Combination Ruler (Stock #8460) behind the shaft as shown in photo 5-27. Mark the shaft for cutting. In this example, the desired final club length is going to be 35 inches. Note the mark is slightly below the final desired club length of 35 inches. Because the end of the grip or grip cap on most grips will account for between $\frac{1}{8}$ inch and $\frac{1}{4}$ inch of the final club length, it is recommended that the shaft be cut slightly below the desired final club length. Once the grip is installed, the final club length is 35 inches.

5-28

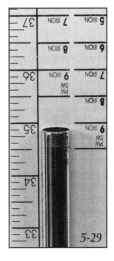

5-29

Remove the head from the shaft and cut the shaft to length. Photo 5-28 shows cutting the shaft using the Stock #858 Super Shaft Cutter. The shaft can also be cut with a 6-inch Cutoff Wheel (Stock #8581) on at least a $\frac{1}{3}$ h.p. motor. See page 33, photo 3-11b for illustration.

With the head on the shaft, re-check the length. Photo 5-29 shows the final cut shaft length at 34 $\frac{7}{8}$ inches.

It's time to epoxy the head onto the shaft. We recommend using the Golfsmith Shafting Epoxy (Stock #9095 for half pint quantity). Parts A and B mix at a 1:1 ratio. It is best to use mixing cups similar to the one pictured. Simply pour out equal amounts of Part A and Part B in separate cups, then mix together. It is very important to mix thoroughly. Mix for at least one minute. Mix until the epoxy is a consistent color throughout (see photo 5-30).

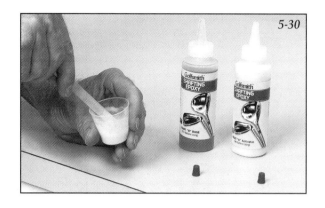

Using a mixing stick, apply the epoxy to the stem on the putter head. Be sure to get good coverage on the entire stem (see photo 5-31).

Also using a mixing stick, apply a small bead of epoxy on the inside of the tip end of the shaft (see photo 5-32).

As an alternative to using the mixing sticks, you can simply dip the stem of the putter head into the epoxy mix. Make sure the stem has an adequate amount of epoxy on it. A thin film on the entire stem is sufficient (see photo 5-33).

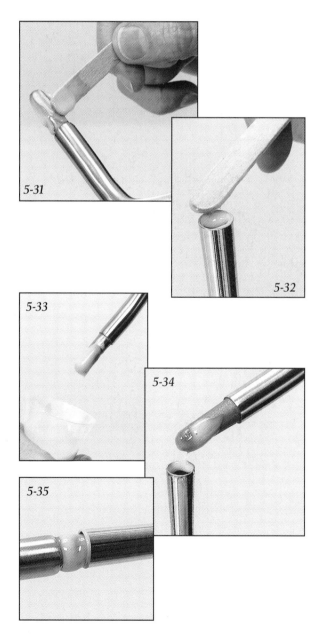

Using the stem, apply a thin bead of epoxy around the inside of the tip end of the shaft (see photo 5-34).

After the epoxy is applied, insert the head stem into the flared tip end of the shaft. To insure you get complete coverage of the epoxy on the stem and shaft, spin the shaft slowly as you put it on the head. Put the shaft all the way on the head, then back it off slightly while rotating the shaft, then put the shaft all the way back onto the head (see photo 5-35). This insures that you get a complete application of the epoxy. Be sure you get the shaft flush up against the top of the hosel. See page 38 for *SPECIAL NOTE:* on epoxy.

5-36

To insure that the shaft is all the way on the head, turn the club upside down and, holding the head in one hand and the shaft in the other, firmly tap the butt of the shaft on a hard surface (see photo 5-36). Remember: do not tap the butt on vinyl, wood or tile floors. A concrete floor, metal block, scrap wood block or similar hard surface is recommended for this procedure.

Using a paper towel, wipe the excess epoxy from around the top of the hosel and off of the shaft. It helps to dampen the towel with an organic grip solvent Wipe as much of the excess epoxy off as possible (see photo 5-37). You should be able to get it completely clean. It is much easier to get this area clean when the epoxy is wet, so be meticulous.

5-37

Photo 5-38 shows how the shaft and head should look after the assembly and cleaning.

Set the club aside to cure in a secure place. Place the head of the club down as shown in photo 5-39.

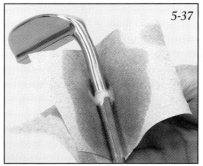

5-38

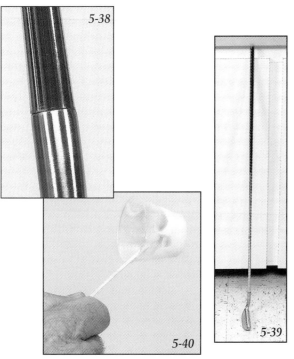

5-40

5-39

After the appropriate time for curing has past (approximately 24 hours), check the mixing cup to see if the mix has cured (see photo 5-40). If the epoxy in the cup appears soft and not cured, do not use the club. Cure rates can vary depending on the outside temperature. At room temperature, 24 hours should be sufficient. Most shafting epoxies are very hard when they cure. If the epoxy is cured correctly, it should appear hard and if pressed firmly with a mixing stick, should leave little, if any indentation.

Check the head for tightness (see photo 5-41).

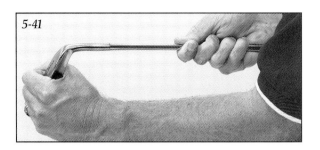
5-41

Install the grip (see photo 5-42). For complete gripping instructions, see Chapter 2.

5-42

INSTALLING BENT PUTTER SHAFTS

One of the more popular putter styles in recent years have been those designed to take putter shafts that are manufactured with varying degrees of bends. Single-bend, double-bend or triple-bend are the terms used to describe the types of shafts used in these types of heads. Mallet head style designs are the most common heads used with these type of shafts. Although a few extra steps are required to assemble these types of putters, it is still a task that can be accomplished with relative ease.

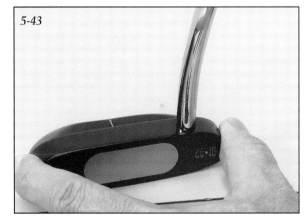
5-43

Test fit the shaft into the head bore (see photo 5-43). Check the bore depth of the hosel with a pencil and note the measurement of the depth. If the shaft slips into the head easily, proceed to the next step. If it does not, it may be necessary to prep the tip of the shaft or remove the chrome from the tip of the shaft first so the shaft will slip into the head (see photo 5-45, 5-45a for shaft prepping procedures). Using the bore depth reference measurement, tape the shaft so that only the portion that will be inside the bore is exposed (as shown in photo 5-44).

If the shaft fits into the head easily, use ¾-inch masking tape and tape off the shaft above the bore (see photo 5-44), right up to the top of the bore. This will mark the shaft for the proper installation depth and protect the shaft during the tip abrading process from scratching above the bore line.

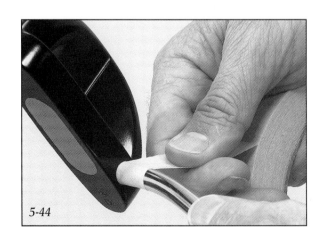
5-44

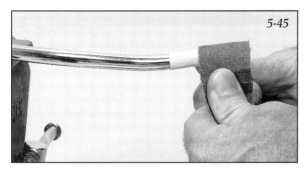

5-45

5-45a

5-45b

Next remove the shaft from the head, and abrade the tip of the shaft. Photo 5-45 shows this process using a medium to coarse grit sandpaper, cut in a one inch strip, being used to rough up the tip of the steel shaft. Place the shaft in a vise using a Protective Rubber Vise Clamp (Stock #913 or Stock #8249) and abrade the tip, being careful not to tear the tape. Photo 5-45a shows the procedure using a 30-inch belt sander (a 42-inch belt sander can also be used) and a medium to coarse grit sanding belt a medium cut file can also be used (not pictured). Whichever method you use, be sure to abrade the entire circumference of the shaft tip. Photo 5-45b shows a close up view of how the shaft tip should look after this procedure is completed.

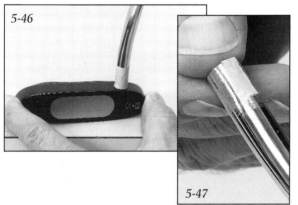

5-46

5-47

Re-check the shaft fit in the head (see photo 5-46).

Before you can install the shaft with epoxy, you must be sure of the positioning of the shaft in the head. The single-, double- and triple-bend shafts must be positioned properly for the putter head to sit square when assembled. To keep the head from moving around freely when trying to position it on the shaft, place a small piece of tape (masking tape will work) on the tip of the shaft (see photo 5-47).

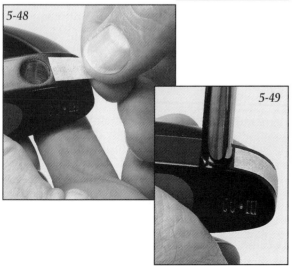

5-48

5-49

Now, place a strip of masking tape on the putter head (see photo 5-48). This is used to mark the shaft position in the head once the shaft is positioned correctly.

Place the shaft into the head (see photo 5-49). The tape on the tip of the shaft should allow you to adjust the head to the right position, but still keep the head from moving freely or falling off the shaft. Photo 5-49a shows how the head should be positioned on the shaft in the playing position.

Notice how the straight part of the shaft is parallel to the face line of the head. Photo 5-49b shows an extreme closed positioning of the head and 5-49c illustrates an extreme open positioning of the head.

Once you have the head and the shaft in the proper position, take a marker and mark the position of the head and the shaft as shown in photo 5-50. It is OK to mark on the chrome portion of the shaft. The mark come off with a little solvent after the assembly. You can simply leave the tape on the shaft from the abrading process and place the mark there if you prefer. These marks identify the correct positioning of the head and will help you align the head and shaft when you are ready to epoxy.

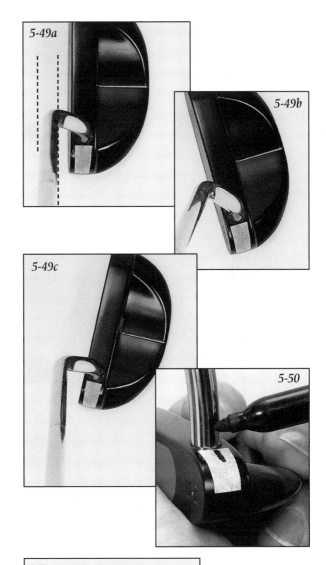

With the head still positioned on the shaft, mark the club for cutting to final length. Because of the bent shaft and the offset of the shaft bend, to properly measure the length, take the 48-inch Combination Ruler (Stock #460) positioning the ruler in front of the face of the putter, running up behind the shaft (see photo 51). Once the ruler is in the position as shown, mark the shaft for length trimming.

Photo 5-52 shows the shaft marked just below the 35-inch mark. This will give a final putter length when assembled with a grip of 35 inches. When marking the shaft for the final length cut, always allow $\frac{1}{8}$ inch to $\frac{1}{4}$ inch for the grip but cap. In this case the shaft is actually cut to 34 $\frac{7}{8}$ inches.

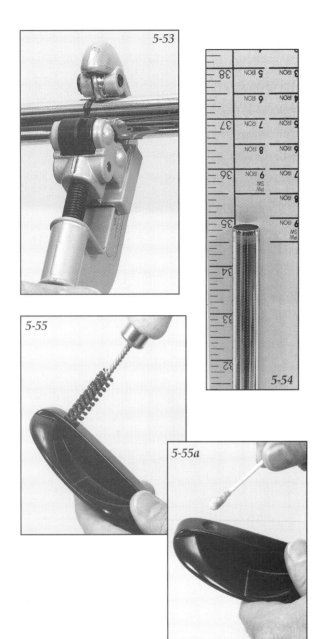

5-53

5-54

5-55

5-55a

Remove the head from the shaft and cut the shaft to length. Photo 5-53 shows cutting the shaft using the Stock #858 Super Shaft Cutter. The shaft can also be cut with a 6-inch cutoff wheel (Stock #8581) on at least a ⅓ h.p. motor. See page 35 in photo 3-11b for illustration.

With the head on the shaft, re-check the length. Photo 5-54 shows the final cut shaft length at 34 ⅞ inches.

Before you can epoxy the shaft into the head, the bore hole in the head must be clean. This is necessary to clean out any dirt, oil or any other kind of contaminant that might prevent the epoxy from bonding the head and shaft together properly. As illustrated in Photo 5-55, the Hosel Cleaner Brush (Stock #8625) is inserted into the bore with a slight twisting motion. This will loosen or remove unwanted material from the bore. It also roughs up the inside of the hosel, which aids in the adhesion of the epoxy. Next, take a cotton swab, dip it into acetone and swab out the inside of the bore (see photo 5-55a). This cleans out all remaining residue. Set the head aside for a few minutes to allow the bore hole to dry.
NOTE: This is a very important step. Most epoxy bond failures are due to contaminants in the epoxy that come from the bore hole.

Before the final assembly with epoxy, we recommend wiping off the abraded portion of the shaft tip with a paper towel dampened with solvent (see photo 5-56). This removes any dust or other particles left on the shaft tip from the abrading process. Be careful not to wipe off the reference mark you put on the shaft to aid in the proper aligning of the head and shaft.

It's time to epoxy the head onto the shaft. We recommend using the Golfsmith Shafting Epoxy (Stock #9095 for half pint quantity). Parts A and B mix at a 1:1 ratio. It is best to use mixing cups similar to the one pictured. Simply pour out equal amounts of Part A and Part B in separate cups, then mix together. It is very

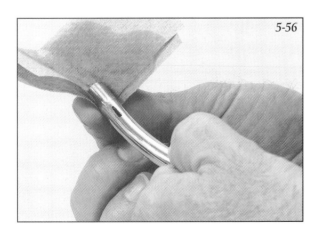

5-56

important to mix thoroughly. Mix for at least a minute until the epoxy is a consistent color throughout (see photo 5-57).

Now install the shaft. Using a mixing stick, put a small bead of epoxy on the inside of the hosel (see photo 5-58). Do not fill the hosel. A small amount is all that is necessary.

Next, take the mixing stick and coat the outside of the tip of the shaft with epoxy (see photo 5-59). Be sure to get a good coverage over the tip of the shaft.

One option, instead of using the mixing stick, is to simply dip the shaft tip into the epoxy mix as shown in photo 5-60. Again, be sure you get good coverage on the outside of the shaft tip.

Once you have thoroughly coated the shaft tip, you can use it to spread the epoxy on the inside of the bore hole (see photo 5-61).

Install the shaft into the head. Rotate the shaft slowly while inserting it into the head. Once it is all the way in, pull it approximately half way out and check to be sure you have complete coverage, and then insert the shaft all the way to the bottom of the bore (see photo 5-62).

Go ahead and clean as much of the epoxy off the head as possible. Use a paper towel or cloth dampened with an organic grip solvent. Remember, it is much easier to get the head and shaft clean when the epoxy is wet. *NOTE: Be very careful not to erase you shaft/head orientation marks* (see photo 5-63).

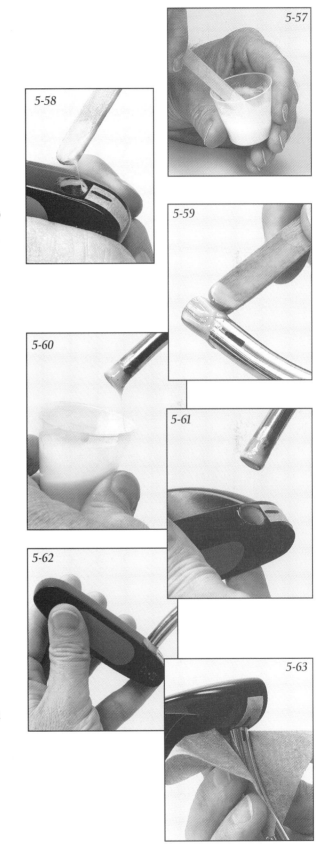

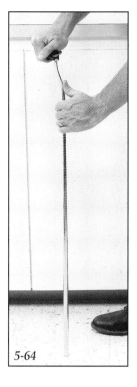

5-64

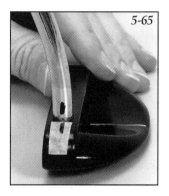

5-65

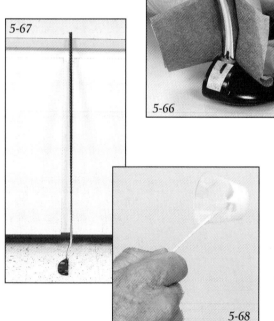

5-66

5-67

5-68

Turn the club upside down and gently tap the butt of the shaft on a hard surface (see photo 5-64). Do not tap the butt on vinyl, wood or tile floors. A concrete floor, metal block or scrap wood block, or a similar hard surface is recommended. This helps insure the shaft is inserted all the way to the bottom of the hosel.

Be sure your designated alignment marks on the head and shaft line up (see photo 5-65).

Clean any more excess epoxy from the head and the shaft (see photo 5-66).

Set the club aside to cure in a secure place. Place the head of the club down as shown in photo 5-67.

After the appropriate time for curing has past (approximately 24 hours), check the mixing cup to see if it has cured (see photo 5-68). If the epoxy in the cup appears soft and not cured, do not use the club. Cure rates can vary depending on the temperature. At room temperature, 24 hours should be sufficient. Most epoxies do not cure rock hard. If the epoxy is cured correctly, it should appear hard and, if pressed firmly with a mixing stick, should leave a slight indention. The Golfsmith 24-hour epoxy will be very hard when it cures. If the epoxy is cured correctly, it should appear hard and if pressed firmly with a mixing stick, should leave little, if any indentation.

SPECIAL NOTE: Outside temperatures can effect the curing time. The warmer it is, the faster and harder the epoxy cures. It is still recommended that no club should be used for a minimum of 24 hours after assembly.

Check the head for tightness (see photo 5-69). Also, if you have not already, remove the tape strip from the head and the alignment mark from the shaft. (Hopefully they are in the same position they were when you set the club aside to dry).

Install the grip (see photo 5-70). For complete instructions on installing grips, see Chapter 2.

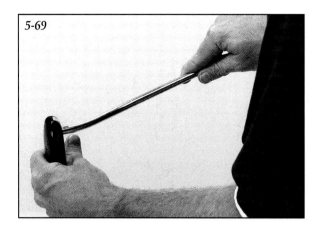

5-69

5-70

Items Needed for Putter Assembly:

- ❏ Golf club components – heads, shafts, grips

- ❏ Organic Grip Solvent

- ❏ ¾-inch or 2-inch two-sided tape

- ❏ Shafting epoxy

- ❏ Mixing cups and sticks

- ❏ Shaft Cutting Tools

    Stock #858 Shaft Cutter or Stock #8581 Cutoff Wheel for steel shafts

    Stock #'s 8587, 8586 Saw Blades or Stock #8581 Cutoff Wheel for graphite shafts

- ❏ Vise Clamps

    Stock #8288 for shaft butts, Stock #8288 for shaft tips and general use

- ❏ 48-inch Combination Ruler – Stock #8460 or Precision Golf Club Rule – Stock #4606

- ❏ Coarse grit sandpaper for prepping steel shafts, surface conditioning belt for graphite shafts

- ❏ Knife for prepping graphite shafts

- ❏ Flex Hone Tool for cleaning hosels, Stock #8625 for irons, Stock #8625 for woods

- ❏ Cotton Swabs - Acetone

- ❏ Bench Vise

- ❏ 30-inch or 42-inch Belt Sander for use in shaft prepping of steel and Graphite shafts- *optional*

- ❏ Epoxy Beads, Stock #9082 - *optional*

WRIST-TO-FLOOR MEASUREMENT CHARTS

DRIVERS

Wrist-To-Floor Measurement	Recommended Driver Length
25" - 27"	41.5"
27" - 29"	42"
29" - 32"	42.5"
32" - 34"	43" (women's std.)
34" - 36"	43.5"
36" - 38"	44" (mens' std.)
38" - 40"	44.5"
40" - 42"	45"
42" and over	45.5"

5-IRONS

Wrist-To-Floor Measurement	Recommended 5-Iron Length
25" - 27"	36"
27" - 29"	36.5"
29" - 32"	37" (women's std.)
32" - 34"	37.5"
34" - 37"	38" (men's std.)
37" - 39"	38.5"
39" - 41"	39"
41" and over	39.5"

Each club in a set should be made one-half inch shorter than the preceding club. For example, a men's set of woods with a 44-inch driver should have a 43.5-inch 2 wood, 43-inch 3 wood, and a 41-inch 5 wood. A men's set of irons with a 39.5-inch 2-iron should have a 39-inch 3 iron, a 38.5-inch 4-iron, a 37-inch 7 iron, and a 36-inch 9 iron. See charts and graphics on page 110-111 for additional information.

NOTE: It is recommended that golf clubs not be shortened increments exceeding one-half inch as the distance a ball is hit is substantially curtailed without a corresponding significant improvement in club control or accuracy.

STANDARD LENGTH, LOFT AND LIE

All specifications below are based on industry averages.

WOODS

CLUB NO.	MEN'S LENGTH	LADIES' LENGTH	LOFT	LIE
#1	44"	43"	10.5°	55°
#2	43.5"	42.5"	13°	55.5°
#3	43"	42"	15°	56°
#4	42.5"	41.5"	17.5°	56.5°
#5	42"	41"	19°	57°
#6	41.5"	40.5"	22°	57.5°
#7	41"	40"	24°	58°
#9	40"	39"	27°	58°
#11	39.5"	38.5"	32°	59°
#13	39"	38"	36°	59.5°
#15	38.5"	37.5"	40°	60°

IRONS

CLUB NO.	MEN'S LENGTH	LADIES' LENGTH	LOFT	LIE
#1	40"	39"	16°	56°
#2	39.5"	38.5"	18°	57°
#3	39"	38"	21°	58°
#4	38.5"	37.5"	24°	59°
#5	38"	37"	27°	60°
#6	37.5"	36.5"	31°	61°
#7	37"	36"	35°	62°
#8	36.5"	35.5"	39°	63°
#9	36"	35"	44°	64°
PW	36"	35"	48°	64°
SW	36"	35"	55°	65°

PUTTERS

Standard Length	
Men's	35" - 36"
Women's	34"

LENGTH, LOFT AND LIE DIAGRAMS

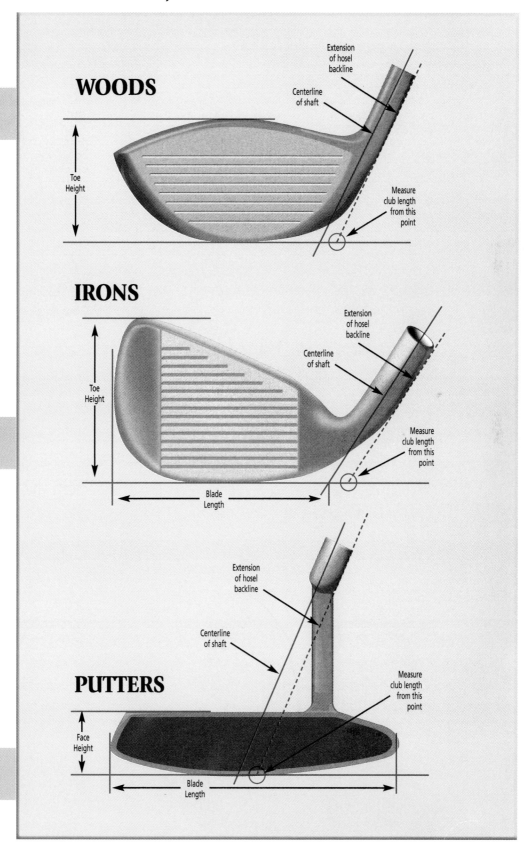

WOODS

Extension
of hosel
backline

Centerline
of shaft

Toe
Height

Measure
club length
from this
point

IRONS

Extension
of hosel
backline

Centerline
of shaft

Toe
Height

Measure
club length
from this
point

Blade
Length

Extension
of hosel
backline

Centerline
of shaft

Measure
club length
from this
point

PUTTERS

Face
Height

Blade
Length

GRIP SIZING CHARTS

Increasing/Decreasing Grip Size

Diameter (inches)
Measured 2" from Butt

	Men's	Ladies'	No. Layers of Build-up Tape
XXX Large (¹/₈" oversize)	1¹/₃₂" (1.020)	3¹/₃₂" (.970)	12
XX Large (¹/₁₆" oversize)	3¹/₃₂" (.960)	2⁹/₃₂" (.910)	6
X Large (¹/₃₂" oversize)	¹⁵/₁₆" (.930)	⁷/₈" (.880)	3
Large (¹/₆₄" oversize)	⁵⁶/₆₄" (.915)	⁵⁵/₆₄" (.865)	1
Standard	²⁹/₃₂" (.900)	²⁷/₃₂" (.850)	0
Small (¹/₆₄" smaller)	⁵⁷/₆₄" (.885)	⁵³/₆₄" (.835)	0**

> **Matching Grip Core Diameter and Shaft Diameter**
> *(ie. M58 on .580 shaft, M60 on .600 shaft, etc.*

*Decimal conversions may not exactly match fractions due to rounding and/or use of accepted industry standards.
**The grip must be stretched an additional ¾" down the shaft to reduce the diameter by ¹/₆₄"

A grip size designation is marked on the inside of the mouth of the grip (see illustration to the left). The letter number designation tells you if the grip is Mens (M) or Ladies' (L) and what the core size is: 58 (.580), 60 (.600), etc.

There may also be the letter "R" following the number, denoting that the grip has a round or non-ribbed construction. If there is no "R", the grip has a rib, sometimes called a reminder, molded in the back side of the grip.

Build-up Layers When Grip Core Size and Shaft Diameter Differ

	Undersize	Standard	Large	X Large	XX Large	XXX Large
M58 → .600/M60 → .620/L56 → .580/L58 → .600	NR	Stretch ¾"	0	1	4	10
M58 → .620	NR	NR	Stretch ¾"	0	2	8
M60 → .580/M62 → .600	NR	2	3	5	8	14
M62 → .580	NR	4	5	7	10	16

CLUBHEAD MATERIALS REFERENCE CHART

Material	Tensile[1] Strength	Yield[1] Strength	Req. Face Thickness[2]	Material Density (g/cc)	Maximum Driver Size[2]	Wt. of 250cc Driver[2]	Elongation[3]	Hardness[4]	Uses
431 Stainless[5]	115	90	n/a	7.6g	n/a	n/a	19%	HRC20	irons only
17-4 Stainless[6]	135	120	3.0mm	7.6g	235cc	215g	15%	HRC36	woods, irons
15-5 Stainless[7]	175	130	2.8mm	7.6g	255cc	198g	14%	HRC40	woods, irons
Maraging Steel	230	210	2.2mm	7.9g	300cc	170g	10%	HRC52	woods, inserts
Carbon Steel	70	40	n/a	7.6g	n/a	n/a	30%	HRB85	irons only
Nickel Alloy[8]	66	45	n/a	8.2g	n/a	n/a	24%	HRB95	irons only
25-5 Elasteel	95	70	n/a	7.6g	n/a	n/a	30%	HRC10	irons
25-5 Elasteel[9]	205	175	variable	7.7g	260cc	210g	12%	HRC43	woods
Aluminum/Bronze	65	55	n/a	7.6g	n/a	n/a	23%	HRB90	irons, putters
A/G Aluminum	70	30	4.8mm	2.8g	350cc	145g	13%	HRB95	woods
Std. Aluminum	25	15	5.5mm	2.8g	300cc	170g	13%	HRB60	woods
6AL-4V Titanium	140	125	3.0mm	4.5g	325cc	160g	8%	HRC34	woods, irons
15-5-3 Beta Titanium	175	160	2.8mm	4.5g	350cc	145g	5%	HRC45	woods
Cermet	105	95	4.5mm	2.7g	370cc	135g	3%	HRC25[10]	woods, irons

1   Measurements on this chart are averages which can be deemed typical for the materials displayed. Final strength measurements can vary depending on the fabrication process and the heat treatment applied to the material. Tensile and yield strengths are listed in 1,000 lbs./in^2, which is also known as ksi.

2   Required Face Thickness, Maximum Driver Size (based on 200-gram weight), and Weight of 250cc Driver all refer to specifications required to produce a driver head capable of withstanding normal wear and tear.

3   Elongation is related to tensile strength and is expressed as a percentage of the change in the material's length after a load is applied and before fracture occurs. The greater the elongation percentage, the tougher and more ductile a material is. Elongation is the most reliable indicator of bendability.

4   Hardness is expressed in the Rockwell Scale which is a test performed to rank materials for their ability to resist penetration of a diamond indenter pressed into the material. The hardness measurement is expressed in a letter and number scale with the higher the letter and number, the harder the material. However, the letter scales do overlap. For example, Rockwell B80 = Rockwell C0; B90 = C10; B100 = C23; B110 = C38. The hardness expressed in this chart is an average and can be changed for most materials depending upon heat treating procedures.

5 Chromium 15%; Nickel 1-2%.   **6** Chromium 17%; Nickel 4%.   **7** Chromium 15%; Nickel 5%.   **8** Nickel 20%.

9   The higher mechanical properties of 25-5 Elasteel for metal woods are made possible by custom heat treatment procedures performed after casting.

10   Cermet's surface hardness rating can be increased to HRC55 through a special nitrogen-cryogenic treatment.

THE GOLFSMITH
Practical Golf
CLUBFITTING PROGRAM

PRELIMINARY FITTING RECOMMENDATION

NAME _____ ADDRESS _____

PHONE Home: (___) _____ Work:(___) _____ CITY _____ STATE _____ ZIP _____

SET MAKEUP   *Circle & write in recommended set makeup*

WOODS   **1 2 3 4 5 7 9** ___ ___ ___ ___

IRONS   **1 2 3 4 5 6 7 8 9** ___ ___ ___

WEDGES   ☐ **PW** ☐ **SW** _____ *Other wedges*

LOFT ANGLES   *Enter recommended loft angles for each*

WOODS   **#1** _____° **#3** _____° **#5** _____° **#__** _____°

IRONS   **#3** _____° **#5** _____° **#7** _____° **#9** _____°

WEDGES   **PW** _____° **SW** _____° ____ _____°

CLUBHEAD DESIGN   *Check all recommended features*

WOODS   ☐ *Jumbo* ☐ *Oversize* ☐ *Mid-size* ☐ *Traditional*

☐ *Steel* ☐ *Aluminum* ☐ *Titanium* ☐ *Graphite* ☐ *Other* _____

☐ *Deep Face* ☐ *Standard Face* ☐ *Shallow Face*   ☐ *Offset* ☐ *Non-offset*   ☐ *Low CG* ☐ *Mid-high CG*

IRONS   ☐ *Cavity Back* ☐ *Muscle Back*   ☐ *Compact* ☐ *Std* ☐ *Oversize*

☐ *Offset* ☐ *Non-offset*   ☐ *Wide Sole* ☐ *Std* ☐ *Thin Sole*

WEDGES   **PW** – ☐ *Wide Sole* ☐ *Medium* ☐ *Thin Sole*   ____ – ☐ *Wide Sole* ☐ *Medium* ☐ *Thin Sole* *(for 3rd or 4th wedge)*

SW – ☐ *Wide Sole* ☐ *Medium* ☐ *Thin Sole*

LENGTH   *List each length; indicate incremental change in length between irons*

WOODS   **1w** _____" **3w** _____" **5w** _____" **#__w** _____" *(for 7w, 9w or other)*

IRONS   **5i** _____" *Incremental Change* _____"   WEDGES **PW** _____" **SW** _____" *Other* ____ ____"

SWINGWEIGHT   *List swing weight for woods & irons*

WOODS _____   IRONS _____   WEDGES **PW** _____ **SW** _____ *Other* _____ ____

TOTAL WEIGHT   *Check driver range; Indicate Fairway woods to match or other by listing shaft weight*

WOODS   **1w** – ☐ *< 11.25 oz.* ☐ *11.25 - 11.75 oz.* ☐ *11.75 - 12.25 oz.* ☐ *12.25 - 12.75 oz.* ☐ *> 12.75 oz.*

Fairway Woods – ☐ *To match to 1w* *Other* _____

IRONS   ☐ *Match Wood Range* *Other* _____

FACE ANGLE   *Check angle*

WOODS   **1w** – _____° ☐ *Hook* ☐ *Square* ☐ *Open*   **Fairway Woods** – _____° ☐ *Hook* ☐ *Square* ☐ *Open*

BULGE/ROLL

WOODS   **1w** – Bulge _____" Roll _____" ☐ *Std*   **Fairway Woods** – Bulge _____" Roll _____" ☐ *Std*

GRIP SIZE   *Check size or indicate other size for woods/irons*

WOODS   ☐ *Jumbo* ☐ *+ 1/16"* ☐ *+ 1/32"* ☐ *+ 1/64"* ☐ *Std.* ☐ *– 1/64"* ☐ *Other* _____

IRONS   ☐ *Jumbo* ☐ *+ 1/16"* ☐ *+ 1/32"* ☐ *+ 1/64"* ☐ *Std.* ☐ *– 1/64"* ☐ *Other* _____

GRIP TYPE/WEIGHT   *Write in grip name and check weight range*

WOODS   *Type* – _____   *Weight* – ☐ *< 40g* ☐ *40-50g* ☐ *>50g*

IRONS   *Type* – _____   *Weight* – ☐ *< 40g* ☐ *40-50g* ☐ *>50g*

SHAFT WEIGHT   *Check shaft weight range and material for each*

WOODS   **1w** – ☐ *< 65g* ☐ *66 - 80g* ☐ *81 - 95g* ☐ *96 - 110g* ☐ *> 110g*   ☐ *Graphite* ☐ *Steel* ☐ *Other*

Fairway Woods – ☐ *< 65g* ☐ *66 - 80g* ☐ *81 - 95g* ☐ *96 - 110g* ☐ *> 110g*   ☐ *Graphite* ☐ *Steel* ☐ *Other*

IRONS   **5i** – ☐ *< 65g* ☐ *66 - 80g* ☐ *81 - 95g* ☐ *96 - 110g* ☐ *> 110g*   ☐ *Graphite* ☐ *Steel* ☐ *Other*

SHAFT FLEX (RSSR) & BEND POINT   *Enter swing speeds - check downswing acceleration; indicate mph range for shaft*

WOODS   **1w** – **Swing Speed** – _____ mph   **Downswing** – ☐ Fast ☐ Avg ☐ Slow   **RSSR** – _____–_____ mph

IRONS   **5i** – **Swing Speed** – _____ mph   **Downswing** – ☐ Fast ☐ Avg ☐ Slow   **RSSR** – _____–_____ mph

WOOD BEND POINT   ☐ *Low* ☐ *Mid/High*   IRON BEND POINT   ☐ *Low* ☐ *Mid/High*

THE GOLFSMITH
Practical Golf CLUBFITTING PROGRAM
EQUIPMENT EVALUATION FORM

NAME _____

ADDRESS _____

CITY _____ STATE _____ ZIP _____

PHONE   Home: (____) _____   Work: (____) _____

HANDICAP/AVG. SCORE _____   HEIGHT _____

WRIST TO FLOOR LENGTH RECOMMENDATION 1w: _____ 5 i: _____

SWING SPEED 1w (3w): _____ mph   5 i: _____ mph

DYNAMIC LIE FITTING ☐ Center of Sole   ☐ _____ " Toward Heel

CURRENT WOODS

Brand/Model: _____

☐ Traditional Size ☐ Offset ☐ Non-offset ☐ Oversize ☐ Mid-oversize ☐ Mid-size

SET MAKEUP	LOFT	FACE ANGLE	TOTAL WEIGHT	SWING WEIGHT	LENGTH	SHAFT MODEL /FLEX	BEND POINT	FREQ.	EST. TORQUE°	RSSR mph
1 ☐										
2 ☐										
3 ☐										
4 ☐										
5 ☐										
6 ☐										
7 ☐										
9 ☐										
___ ☐										
___ ☐										

SHAFT WEIGHT DRIVER
☐ Heavy 110g +
☐ Medium 96-110g
☐ Light 81-95g
☐ Very Light 66-80g
☐ Ultra Light 50-65g

WOODS GRIP SIZE
☐ Undersize ___ / ___ "
☐ Std. Men's/Ladies
☐ + 1/64
☐ + 1/32
☐ + 1/16
☐

Grip Type: _____

CURRENT IRONS

Brand/Model: _____

☐ Offset ☐ Non-offset ☐ Prog.Offset ☐ Oversize ☐ Mid-size ☐ Compact ☐ Cavity Back ☐ Muscle

SET MAKEUP	LOFT	TOTAL WEIGHT	SWING WEIGHT	LENGTH	SHAFT MODEL /FLEX	BEND POINT	FREQ.	EST. TORQUE°	RSSR mph
1 ☐									
2 ☐									
3 ☐									
4 ☐									
5 ☐									
6 ☐									
7 ☐									
8 ☐									
9 ☐									
PW ☐ (10)									
SW ☐									
___ ☐									
PT ☐									

SHAFT WEIGHT 5-IRON
☐ Heavy 110g +
☐ Medium 96-110g
☐ Light 81-95g
☐ Very Light 66-80g
☐ Ultra Light 50-65g

IRONS GRIP SIZE
☐ Undersize ___ / ___ "
☐ Std. Men's/Ladies
☐ + 1/64
☐ + 1/32
☐ + 1/16
☐

Grip Type: _____

SOLE ANGLE
_____ °   ☐ Sq.

Bounce

Custom Loft & Lie Adjustments

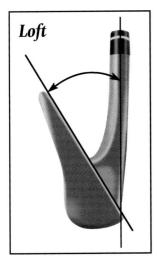

Golfsmith's craftsmen can bend most iron heads to your specifications, enabling precision clubfitting. In addition, we now have the technology in our shop to bend most metal wood heads for lie angle and face angle. The work is performed to exacting specifications on our professional equipment. Iron heads may be bent for Loft (strong or weak) or Lie (flat or upright).

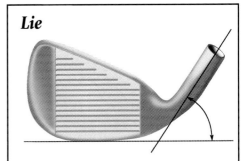

BIH   BEND IRON HEADS for Loft/Lie (per head) $3.00

IMPORTANT NOTE: *The bending process occasionally will leave a slight nick or mar in the clubhead that will in no way affect playability. Heads made of 431, 17-4 or 15-5 stainless may be bent a maximum of 2°; nickel iron heads up to 4°. NOT BENDABLE for loft and lie are short-hosel or no-hosel metal wood heads, or any heads made of titanium, ti-alloy, cermet or duraluminum. Refer to specification charts in the Golfsmith Components Catalog to determine clubhead material.*
ALSO: *Clubheads made of 17-4 or 15-5 stainless are considered "not bendable" for most clubmakers because they require special bending equipment.*

Golfsmith Iron Heads' Lifetime Warranty

Golfsmith offers the widest selection of iron heads in the golf industry, precision manufactured with some of the tightest metallurgical specifications in the industry. Our forged or investment cast iron heads carry a lifetime warranty. This limited warranty covers any material or manufacturing defects. Simply return the defective clubhead at any time for repair, replacement or refund. Does not apply to normal wear and tear, or to heads damaged due to misuse, abuse or alteration.

GLOSSARY

15-5 STAINLESS – An ultra-hard form of stainless steel with 15% chromium content which has a higher yield strength and tensile strength than 431 and 17-4. It also has a higher Rockwell hardness rating than 431 and 17-4 stainless.

17-4 – Stainless steel of a specific composition – 17% Chromium and 4% Nickel – used in casting metal wood heads; 17-4 is not easily bendable.

431 STAINLESS – Stainless steel of a special composition – about 15 % chromium and less than 1 % nickel – used in casting iron or metal wood heads; 431 is not easily bendable.

ACETONE – A clear chemical used in golf club-making to soften or shape plastic parts such as ferrules.

ADDRESS – Positioning the club behind the ball with the intention of hitting it.

ANGLE OF ATTACK – The angle formed by the clubhead approaching the ball and the groundline.

ARAMID FIBERS – Shock absorbing synthetic material that is used in the manufacture of composite shafts for added strength. Frequently known by their brand names such as Kevlar or Spectra, these fibers are also used in making bulletproof vests.

BACKWEIGHTING – The process of adding weight to the butt end of a golf club. This increases the overall weight of the club, but reduces the swing-weight of the club.

BEND POINT – The position on a shaft that exhibits the greatest amount of bending when the bend is achieved by compressing the shaft from one or both ends. Also known as flex point.

BLADE – Long, flat portion of the club used to strike the ball.

BLADE LENGTH – The distance from the toe to the heel of the hosel at a point about ⅓ up the face.

BORON – A synthetic fiber with twice the strength and stiffness as steel, used primarily for tip – reinforcement in graphite shafts. The boron is typically placed in a shaft in a thin ring around the tip diameter, close to the shaft core.

BOUNCE – see Sole Angle.

BULGE – A measure of the curvature of a wood face horizontally expressed as a portion of the radius of a circle. Also, a section on a shaft that swells in diameter, such as the section below the grip on the Taylor Made Bubble shafts. The bulge is used in the design of the shaft to change the location of the bending of the shaft.

BUTT – The grip end of a golf shaft.

CAMBER – The radius of a curvature from heel to toe in the sole of an iron head.

CARBON FIBER – A strong, non-metallic, light-weight fiber created through a heat-induced chemical change. Graphite.

CENTER BALANCED – A putter design feature that positions the weight of the head equally between the toe and the heel in relation to the shaft line. A putter is considered center balance if you can hold the putter across your index finger in a position parallel to the ground and the face of the putter points straight up and is also parallel to the ground.

CENTER OF GRAVITY – Used primarily to describe the playability of the clubhead, center of gravity is one point of balance of the clubhead that is controlled by head size and location of head weight. The lower the center of gravity, the easier the club gets the club airborne. Also the farther back the center of gravity is back from the face, the easier the gets the ball airborne.

COMBINATION FLEX – Refers to a unitized, parallel tip shaft that may be trimmed to achieve one of two flexes, such as R/S (Regular/Stiff) or L/A (Ladies/A-Flex) combination. In general, the more you trim from the tip of the shaft, the stiffer the shaft will play.

COMPOSITE – The joining of two or more materials to create a shaft. Graphite, Boron, fiberglass, ceramic, titanium, amorphous material and Kevlar are other materials that are combined with resin binding agents to create composite shafts. The term composite is sometimes used interchangeably with graphite, but is more inclusive.

CURING – A heat-treating process necessary to change the properties of materials used in making an alloy or composite shaft. Also, a term to describe the epoxy drying process during assembly.

DEEP FACE – A standard wood head face is 1 ⅝ inches from the sole to the top line of the insert. A head that is greater in depth is said to be a deep face.

DEFLECTION – The amount of bend in a shaft when a known force is suspended from the tip. One of the predominant methods for identifying shaft flex.

DYNAMIC LIE – The angle formed by the centerline and the groundline of the club at impact. The lie of the club at impact.

EPOXY – A two-part resin consisting of a base and activator. When mixed it can be used for bonding, casting or molding.

FACE – The surface of a golf club specifically intended for hitting the ball.

FACE ANGLE – On a wood head, the angle in degrees between the face and the target line when it rests on the ground. Also, in the golf swing, the angle that the face points when impact occurs with the ball.

FACE CENTERLINE – An imaginary line through the center of the clubface.

FACE DEPTH – A measure of the height of a wood face from top to bottom. A standard wood face is approximately 1 ⅝ inches in depth.

FERRULE – A tapered sleeve, usually black plastic, used to make a smooth transition between the shaft and the wood or iron hosel (neck).

FILAMENT WINDING – A process of manufacturing a seamless composite shaft by wrapping a continuous "string" or "yarn" of resin-impregnated graphite material around a forming mandrel. Filament winding is an alternative to traditional "sheet-wrapped" graphite shaft manufacture.

FLANGE – Term describing the elongation of the trailing edge of an iron or a putter. The lower back edge of an iron or putter is loosely referred to as the flange.

FLAG – Term used to describe a single sheet of composite graphite material, which is cut into the pennant shape to wrap around the forming mandrel. As many as a dozen flags can be used to make a composite shaft. Also known as Ply.

FLAT – Describes a lie angle for any clubhead, which is lower than normal for that particular numbered clubhead.

FLEX – The relative stiffness or overall bending property of a shaft. Flex is identified by the manufacturers by checking on a deflection board or by the frequency oscillation method. Within a single pattern or design of shafts flex usually related to weight.

FORGING – A method of forming iron heads or metal wood heads.

FREQUENCY – The rate of vibration of a shaft as measured in the number of oscillations over a known period of time. Frequency is used as a way to measure and identify shaft flex. Shaft frequency is most often expressed in the number of cycles per minute (CPM). The higher the CPM reading, the stiffer the flex of the shaft.

GRAPHITE – White Poly Acrile Nitrate (PAN) fibers are heated to create black carbon filaments that are called graphite fibers. The graphite fibers can be mixed with resins and formed into pre-prepreg sheets or combined together in strand form to make graphite shafts. See Composite. In its raw form, graphite is also used in making lead pencils and bearing lubricants.

GRIT – The texture or coarseness of a sanding medium.

HEEL – That portion of a wood or iron head closest to the golfer when the club is held in a hitting position.

HEEL-TOE WEIGHTING – The process of distributing the weight of a wood or iron head toward the toe and heel.

HOSEL – The neck of an iron head or wood head.

IN-HOSEL – A shaft-to-iron head hosel assembly where the shaft fits inside the hosel.

INVESTMENT CASTING – A process of molding metal products, usually from stainless steel.

KICK POINT – A measurement of the shaft's chief point of bending when the shaft is deflected under a known force pulling down on the tip end.

LAUNCH ANGLE – The angle in degrees that the ball takes off from the face at impact.

LIE – The angle formed by the centerline of the shaft and groundline, with the club properly soled.

LOFT – The angle formed by a line drawn parallel to the clubface and a line drawn along the centerline of the shaft and hosel.

LORYTHMIC SCALE – A type of swingweight scale measuring swingweight about a fulcrum point 14 inches down from the top of the grip. Measurements are in direct letter/number (alphanumeric) swingweight designation such a D1, D2, D3.

LOST WAX – A method of producing iron heads or metal wood heads by casting also called Investment Casting. Wax positives are made from a master mold, then dipped repeatedly into a ceramic/sand mixture to form a negative shell. The wax is then melted and drained (hence the term "lost wax") and the molten stainless steel poured in.

MANDREL – The steel-forming rod around which the graphite material is wrapped or wound to make a composite shaft. The mandrel is removed once the composite materials have been cured, thus creating the core of the shaft.

MASTER – The original model(s) from which the head(s) in a set will be duplicated.

MMC (METAL MATRIX COMPOSITE) – Any metal made from a combination of ceramic particles and a single metal. The ceramic particles greatly increase the original metal's strength.

MODULUS – A description of any material's resistance to stretching. In graphite fibers, the modulus rating expresses the proximity of how close the carbon atoms align in the molecular structure, thus creating a stronger bond.

MOMENT OF INERTIA – The measurement of the clubhead's ability to resist twisting. The higher the moment of inertia, the more the clubhead is able to resist twisting. Greater moment of inertia = greater perimeter weighting = more solid feel on off-center shots.

OEM – Original equipment manufacturer, as in the name brand golf venders who sell finished products.

OFFSET – Usually refers to the distance from the centerline of the hosel to the leading edge of a golf clubhead.

OVERALL WEIGHT – The actual weight of a complete club; also called "dead" or "static" weight.

OVERHOSEL – A shaft-to-clubhead assembly in which the shaft fits over the hosel or a protrusion of the hosel.

PARALLEL TIP – Refers to shafts that are the same diameter for a specific distance up from the tip. This distance is called the shaft's parallel section.

PERIMETER WEIGHTING – A weighting process whereby most of the weight of a golf club head is placed on the outermost edges.

PREPREG – Graphite/fiber material mixed with binder resins and formed into thin sheets. Prepreg sheets are used exclusively in the manufacture of sheet wrapped composite shafts.

PRORYTHMIC SCALE – A swingweight scale that also gives the total weight of a club.

RECOMMENDED SWING SPEED RANGE (RSSR) – An independent rating of the overall playing characteristics of the shaft, expressed in miles per hour.

ROLL – The vertical curvature or radius in the face of a wood.

SCORING – Thin lines in the face of a wood or iron head.

SHAFT CLAMP – a device, usually made of rubber or with a rubber lining used as a protective device designed to hold the shaft in a vise without damaging the shaft.

SHAFT FLEX – The measurement of a shaft's resistance to bending.

SOLE – The bottom of a wood or iron. That portion of the head that touches the ground.

SOLE ANGLE – On an iron or wedge, the sole angle represents the angle of the sole line to the ground.

SOLE RADIUS – The two curvatures of the sole, from toe-to-heel and from front-to-back.

STATIC WEIGHT – The actual total weight of a golf club.

STEP PATTERN – The size, numbers, and pattern of steps in a steel shaft.

STEPS – A point at which a steel golf shaft is reduced in diameter from butt to tip.

STRONG – Describes a clubheads loft angle which is smaller or less than normal for that particular numbered clubhead.

SWEET SPOT – The location of the area or "spot" considered to give the most solid impact with the ball.

SWINGPATH – The actual line on which the club-head travels through impact with the ball as compared to a line traveling straight through the ball to the target. Swing path descriptions are described as inside-to-outside, square, or outside-to-in.

SWINGWEIGHT – A letter-number designation of the weight distribution of a golf club. Also, the measure of the balance of a golf club.

TAPERED SHAFT – A wood or iron golf shaft in which the diameter tapers smaller at the tip end.

TIP OR BUTT DIAMETER – The distance from one side of the shaft tip or butt to the other, which affects tip strength, torque in some cases, overall shaft weight, grip size and clubhead installation.

TITANIUM – A lightweight, high-strength metal alloy used in the manufacture of clubheads and shafts.

TORQUE – The amount, in degrees, a shaft twists when a known amount of force is applied to the tip. Torque is measured by securing the butt and applying a force to twist the tip end of the shaft. Torque readings are unique to each manufacturer since each may measure this characteristic differently.

TOE – The outward point of a wood or iron club-head as it is held in the hitting position. Also, the point of the clubhead farthest from the golfer.

TOTAL WEIGHT – The actual weight of the golf club as expressed in ounces or grams.

UNDERLISTING – Serves as the foundation on the shaft butt for a leather or synthetic rubber wrap style grip.

UNITIZED SHAFT – Shafts that are of a single raw length, usually with a parallel tip, which are tip and/or butt trimmed in increments to achieve the proper step pattern or shaft-to-shaft flex relationship within the set.

UPRIGHT – Describes a lie angle for any clubhead, which is higher than normal for that particular numbered head.

VENT HOLE – The hole in the butt end of a rubber grip that releases air pressure during gripping.

VISE PADS – Padded holders, usually wooden or rubber that protect a club finish from scarring while clamped in a vise.

WEAK – Describes a clubheads loft angle which is greater than normal for that particular numbered clubhead.